Praise for *Dreams*

"Muslim hearts are opening through powerful dreams of Jesus. Our Savior loves them and is reaching out to them with His grace and forgiveness. The real revolution in the Middle East is the Jesus Revolution that is occurring today. Tom Doyle has thrilling accounts of Muslims coming to faith in Christ in his new book *Dreams and Visions*."

"R", A FORMER MUSLIM IMAM IN THE MIDDLE EAST (NOW A FOLLOWER OF JESUS)

"Tom Doyle is an expert on church planting in the Middle East. He has his finger on the pulse of a region desperately seeking God. Tom's ministry is fruitful because he understands Islam, has a deep love for Muslims, and knows how to reach out to them with the Gospel effectively."

HORMOZ SHARIAT, IRAN ALIVE MINISTRIES

"Something powerful is happening in the Middle East, and I don't mean the so-called Arab Spring. The *real* news is that record numbers of people in the Muslim world are coming to faith in Jesus Christ! In this stirring book, you will read how the Lord is using what some might think are unusual methods to draw people to Him, but nothing is impossible with God. You won't be able to read this book without your heart racing with joyous excitement about the real revolution in the Arab world."

JANET PARSHALL, NATIONALLY SYNDICATED TALK SHOW HOST

"In *Dreams and Visions* Tom Doyle lifts the veil on the Muslim world. Jesus is on the move and He's visiting Muslims worldwide! Unseen and too often under reported, Muslims coming to faith in Jesus Christ through dreams and visions is a modern-day spiritual earthquake. You can't understand today's Middle East completely without knowing about this supernatural phenomenon."

CHRIS MITCHELL, CBN NEWS MIDDLE EAST BUREAU CHIEF

"Tom and JoAnn Doyle are personal friends. The stories they have relayed to me over the years are thrilling, and reaffirm that God loves the entire world . . . not just Jews and Christians, Israelis and Americans . . . so much that He has just given us Jesus! Their stories have warmed my heart, stretched my faith, broadened my perspective, and put me on my knees in prayer for the Good News of God's love to penetrate the hearts of people everywhere."

ANNE GRAHAM LOTZ, AUTHOR OF *The Magnificent Obsession* AND *Expecting to See Jesus*

"*Dreams and Visions* is another powerful work from the pen of Tom Doyle. In this book Tom takes us on a tour of the Muslim world to reveal how God is bringing men and women to faith in Jesus as their Savior. His frontline stories are compelling and convicting—compelling because they open our eyes to the amazing way God is at work in the Muslim world . . . and convicting because they force us to evaluate the depth of our own spiritual fervor for Christ. Buy the book . . . and pray your way through it!"

DR. CHARLES DYER
PROFESSOR-AT-LARGE OF BIBLE AT THE MOODY BIBLE INSTITUTE
HOST OF *The Land and the Book* RADIO PROGRAM

"*Dreams and Visions* is a must-read book. I believe that today we are living in the beginning days of Joel 2:28. Old men are dreaming dreams and young men are seeing visions. It may shock you, but Muslims are experiencing 'Jesus visits' and eventually many of them are becoming dedicated followers."

KAMAL SALEEM, AUTHOR OF *The Blood of Lambs: A Former Terrorist's Memoir of Death and Redemption*

"Tom's book has encouraged me to pray more for my Muslim neighbors and have faith that no barrier or regime can stop the hand of God from working in the region! May this book and the moving testimonies it tells of Muslims coming to faith do the same for you!"

SAMUEL SMADJA, PASTOR—JERUSALEM
OWNER/PRESIDENT, SAR-EL TOURS & CONFERENCES, ISRAEL

"Tom Doyle brings us amazing insight with his new book *Dreams and Visions*. Through his many years of serving on the front lines in the Middle East and North Africa, he has compiled these recent and genuine accounts of how the one true God is getting his message of love to a people that have been captives for centuries by a suffocating religious system. Jesus is reaching out to Muslims and they are responding. You will be moved and inspired by the exciting stories of the many 'Jesus visits' in *Dreams and Visions!*"

JASON ELAM, ISRAEL DIRECTOR FOR E3 PARTNERS
FORMER NFL ALL-PRO KICKER FOR THE DENVER
BRONCOS AND THE ATLANTA FALCONS

"Tom Doyle shares true stories about the glorious and historic flood of Muslims coming to Jesus in the Middle East and around the world. Welcome to a world you may have never heard about or experienced."

ARTHUR BLESSITT
Guinness World Records FOR CARRYING THE CROSS
IN EVERY NATION OF THE WORLD

"Few groups are as misunderstood and misrepresented by today's followers of Jesus as Muslims. They are often feared by Christians—and regrettably even hated. Thankfully, Jesus loves, and so does Tom Doyle. He unapologetically and irrevocably extends his hand to all. I have personally seen his ministry in the Middle East up close. It is quite possible that Muslims represent the greatest harvest of the Great Commission. *Dreams and Visions* shatters common misperceptions with a simple truth—Jesus is leading the way. I highly recommend this book."

DR. ROY L. PETERSON
PRESIDENT AND CEO, THE SEED COMPANY

"God is shaking the foundations of this world, and the biggest upheaval is taking place in the Arab world. Family dynasties are being overthrown, and the political landscape is changing in the Middle East. It is being chronicled daily in the secular media, but the news is not able to understand what is happening in the spiritual realm. My friend Tom Doyle will sort it all out for you. Tom is a major player in an exciting drama being acted out in the Middle East. You will be thrilled and challenged to hear how Muslims all over the Islamic world are coming to faith in Christ. And many times, it all begins with a dream about Jesus. Hang on to your seat for this book will take you on an exciting ride!"

DR. NEIL T. ANDERSON, FOUNDER AND PRESIDENT
EMERITUS OF FREEDOM IN CHRIST MINISTRIES

"There are thousands of people who are receiving supernatural dreams and visions throughout the Middle East, but very few have heard the actual stories. Tom Doyle has traveled extensively through these countries and written a powerful and riveting first-hand account of their experiences. Their testimonies are like the Bible coming alive. I know, for I have had the privilege of traveling with Tom and meeting some of our newest brothers and sisters. This book will transport you into the land of miracles, and ignite a fire in your soul!"

RAY BENTLEY, SENIOR PASTOR OF MARANATHA CHAPEL, SAN DIEGO, CA

"Tom Doyle is the real deal! I have traveled with him overseas and seen first-hand his remarkable love for lost people, displaced people, for Muslims and Jews. Tom is absolutely right; God is doing something special around the Muslim world right now! May God give us the grace to step into the fray, pray like crazy and lift up Christ, who alone brings redemption, reconciliation, eternal life, and hope."

ROB BUGH, SENIOR PASTOR OF WHEATON BIBLE CHURCH, CHICAGO, IL

"I feel somewhat personally responsible for this book! I've been telling Tom for years, 'Dude, you've got to put all these great stories you share on my show in a book so people beyond LA can hear what God is doing in the Muslim world!' And, I'm jealous . . . there're stories in here I haven't heard before! Tom, what's up with that? Love ya, bro. Congratulations!"

FRANK PASTORE, RADIO TALK SHOW HOST, 99.5 FM KKLA, LOS ANGELES

"Dreams and Visions will rock your world. This account of God's dramatic supernatural work among Muslims will shock most people. While biblical and balanced, Tom Doyle relates what yet seems fantastic to those unfamiliar with what God is doing around His world today."

CURTIS V. HAIL, PRESIDENT OF E3 PARTNERS & I AM SECOND

"These incredible stories of courage and faith in the midst of true suffering remind us that the Book of Acts is alive and well today, and that there are still those who are willing to die for the One who died for them. Through compelling testimonies of God's extraordinary power and love, Tom takes us past our fears and misconceptions of the Muslim world and gives us hope that the impossible is really possible. He outlines a historical and theological premise for God's movement among Muslims today, and reminds us that they are people that God deeply loves and longs to know. Tom challenges us to get up and step out into the greatest assignment in all the earth—the task of testifying to the Gospel of the grace of God. An inspirational and relevant read for anyone who has ever wondered how to build a bridge and engage his Muslim neighbor."

HEATHER MERCER, GLOBAL HOPE PRESIDENT
AUTHOR OF *Prisoners of Hope: The Story of
Our Captivity and Freedom in Afghanistan*

DREAMS
and
VISIONS

IS JESUS AWAKENING THE
MUSLIM WORLD?

TOM DOYLE
with Greg Webster

W PUBLISHING GROUP

AN IMPRINT OF THOMAS NELSON

Published in Nashville, Tennessee, by W Publishing Group, an imprint of Thomas Nelson. Thomas Nelson is a registered trademark of HarperCollins Christian Publishing, Inc.

Thomas Nelson titles may be purchased in bulk for educational, business, fund-raising, or sales promotional use. For information, please e-mail SpecialMarkets@ThomasNelson.com.

Unless otherwise noted, Scripture quotations in this book are taken from the Holy Bible, New International Version®, NIV®. Copyright © 1973, 1978, 1984, 2011 by Biblica, Inc.™ Used by permission of Zondervan. All rights reserved worldwide. www.zondervan.com.

Scripture quotations marked NKJV are taken from *The Holy Bible*, New King James Version (NKJV). Copyright © 1979, 1980, 1982 by Thomas Nelson, Inc. Used by permission. All rights reserved.

Library of Congress Cataloging-in-Publication Data

ISBN 978-0-8499-4720-9

Doyle, Tom.
  Dreams and visions : is God awakening the Muslim world? / Tom Doyle, with Greg Webster.
      p. cm.
  Includes bibliographical references.
  ISBN 978-0-8499-4720-9 (trade paper)
  1. Christian converts from Islam--Biography. 2. Christianity and other religions--Islam. 3. Islam--Relations--Christianity. I. Webster, Greg. II. Title.
  BV2626.3.D69 2012
  261.2'7--dc23

2012020333

Printed in the United States of America

16 17 18 19 RRD 29

Contents

Contents

Contents

*I revealed myself
to those who did not ask for me;
I was found
by those who did not seek me.*

—Isaiah 65:1

To Jesus~

*You are the King of the Universe and my
savior. How amazing You are! We live in days
of accelerated global transformation and social
unrest, yet You remain the rock of our salvation
and the anchor of our hope.*

I love you.

*"In this world you will have trouble. But take
heart! I have overcome the world."*

John 16:33

Jesus and Muslims

The world appears to be getting more dangerous by the minute. Sometimes it seems as if the "tares" sown in the Master's field are taking over.[1] Yet there is a God in heaven who still cares about us, still sits on His throne, and still has a plan. And thanks to His revolutionary plan for our world, the wheat is flourishing.

The world-shattering tactics of God exhibit an ebb and flow, and church historians have a word for these periods of revolution: *revivals*. In each revival, God moves, Jesus is lifted up, people repent, and cultures are transformed. Nations and continents have been shaken by the power of these fresh works of God, but today's movement may be the most startling of all time. It will likely have the most far-reaching effect on the world since Jesus first set foot in our dimension more than two thousand years ago. These days, Jesus is introducing Himself to Muslims.

The phenomenon is not limited to a few isolated locations. It's not happening in just one or two African nations. There's not just one of several hundred people groups affected in India. He's not simply visiting some lucky town in the Middle East. What we see is Jesus presenting Himself to Muslims everywhere. Dozens of Islamic countries and countless Muslim cultures have been invaded by Jesus' love.

If you are concerned about the end of the world or Islamic fundamentalism or whether or not America will survive an economic collapse, this book is for you. Whatever world condition worries you most, you can take heart that Jesus remains firmly in control.

As always, Jesus touches people one by one. This book presents a handful of the thousands of personal stories you won't be hearing on the news. Yet it reveals the most important movement of our time—the movement of God.

So take a deep breath and enter a new world. Muslims are coming to faith in Jesus all over the globe. Their faith is fresh, and their passion will capture your heart. Your new brothers and sisters in Christ live in Iran, Afghanistan, Egypt, Saudi Arabia, and the Gaza Strip. They make their homes in Syria, Jordan, Iraq, and the West Bank. And everywhere, they are bold and willing to die for Christ.

Each of their stories is really His story. Jesus wants you to know what He's doing and to appreciate the power by which He still works today. To us, these dreams and visions are supernatural experiences, but to Jesus, I suspect He's just doing business here on earth the way He always has. The stories in this book are about real people I know personally or are known by my family's closest friends in the Middle East. If we couldn't verify the experience, we left it out—no Christian fairy tales here.

More Muslims are coming to faith in Jesus today than ever before. In fact, we believe more Muslims have become followers of Jesus in the last ten years than in the last fourteen centuries of Islam. Could it be that the *real* story about Muslims today is not global terrorism? Could it be the real story about Muslims is that Jesus is reaching out to them with His offer of eternal life earned by His death on the cross and resurrection from the dead? I believe Islamic terrorism is Satan's attempt to keep the gospel message away from Muslims. The enemy thinks that if he can make the rest of us afraid of Muslims or make us hate them, then he can short-circuit Jesus' church from reaching Muslims. But that isn't working. Jesus has stepped in and is opening Muslim hearts Himself.

In order to protect the courageous believers who are willing to let me share their stories, I've changed some names and a few details that could reveal identities and put people in even greater danger than the threats they already face. But make no mistake, these are actual stories of believers on the front lines. You'll see this is far more exciting than the best fiction. The real stuff God does is much more interesting. So prepare to be amazed. Islam has a visitor. Jesus has arrived.

PART · I

EGYPT—HOSANNA TO THE KING OF THE ARABS

ONE

Friday at the Khan

Y ou're the one!" A woman's shout broke above the pandemonium of Cairo's Khan el-Khalili Friday Market. "You're the one!"

Kamal Assam spun toward the voice. His eyes fixed on the black hijab walking toward him. A female hand protruded from the full-body covering, pointing in his direction.

"Yes! You!"

Instincts begged him to ignore this culturally dangerous assault and dissolve into the crowd. If the woman's husband were anywhere near and saw her approach, she—and likely Kamal—would pay a steep price for this outburst. Kamal couldn't fathom why an observant Muslim woman would choose today to potentially ruin his life. Then a calmer voice inside suggested this might be the very reason Kamal had made his unusual trip to the marketplace.

"You were in my dream last night." The woman, now close enough to be heard without shouting, breathed heavily from the effort of pushing through the mob and from her own shock at the unfolding mystery of her circumstances.

"Those clothes. You were wearing those clothes. For sure, it is you."

Kamal instantly recognized why this person had so passionately invaded his life. "Was I with Jesus?" he asked.

"Yes," the woman cried, "Jesus was with us!"

What had begun as an atypical visit for him to the Friday Market had just taken an even more uncanny and exciting turn. That morning while reading his Bible, Kamal felt a compelling urge to leave the house where he was staying and venture to the Friday Market. At the heart of Egypt's capital city, the Khan el-Khalili is as much an arena as a marketplace. A Mamluk prince built it in 1382, and in some places it smells that old. No ordinary souk (marketplace), this massive outdoor mall is next to the famed Hussein mosque and even has a hotel for those who want to mix religion with shopping. Whether a kitchen utensil, sumac spice, or pair of Nike knockoffs, most anything—legal and otherwise—is sold there.

A short walk from the Khan stands Al-Azhar University, the oldest degree-granting university in Egypt and the chief center for Sunni Islam worldwide. For Arab Muslims, this is the promised land and the reason that a suicide bomber detonated himself in the middle of the Khan on April 7, 2007.

The attack was a response to the government's treatment of another group of terrorists that had bombed the Hilton Taba by the Red Sea in the Sinai Peninsula on the same day in 2004. In that attack, thirty-one Jews were left dead.

The terrorist act in April 2007 sent a message to the government: stay out of any dealings with Jews. As a result of the bombing in the capital of Sunni Islam, from then on no place in Cairo was considered safe. Tourism in Egypt collapsed—at least for a while.

But now the hordes were back. Tourists weren't thinking of terrorist attacks. They focused on getting a good deal on some fine pashmina goat's wool without getting a wallet lifted in between negotiations with a local merchant. Any tourist who dared enter the Khan would be fortunate to leave with only the money spent on trinkets missing from his or her person. The poor of Cairo "shop" here, a population that includes some of the world's most skilled pickpockets. And only veteran locals with calloused olfactory sense can long endure the stench. Most of the items are secondhand—some stolen—but the bargains are irresistible, so consumers, indigenous and tourist alike, endure the tidal wave of unpleasantness. Fistfights and brawls are common. Shoppers create their own paths through the chaos of merchandise, animals, and human beings, jostling other marketgoers out of the way to achieve their buying goals.

The senseless layout reflects all of life in Cairo, like the downtown motor traffic where eight rows of cars cram into three lanes. Neither the drivers there nor the clientele on foot in the market have any hope of maintaining full control of where they go.

The market's entertainment options are as bizarre as its product offerings. Fire-eaters and magicians compete with card-trick artists and glass eaters for an audience. And human forms in alien costumes with no discernible purpose roam among the thousands of Muslim men and women frantically shopping to complete their secular business before Friday prayers shut down commerce for the rest of the day.

A Veiled Woman and a Single Man

So why would Kamal brave this Friday free-for-all? Only the most urgent of necessities ever compelled him to attend, and even then, he avoided the central market area by using one of the less-thriving entryways. But this particular Friday, he went because God told him to go. He knew with 100 percent certainty God had an assignment waiting for him there. The details of the mission were a mystery to him, but he was used to trusting God in the face of the unknown.

So when the market opened at 8 a.m., Kamal was there. He had briefly resisted the urge to avoid the central market and visit the relatively less mobbed areas he preferred—if anything could be "preferred" about the marketplace—but he yielded even that desire to what he knew was God's prompting and found himself crushed and battered by the crowd while he waited for he wasn't sure what.

That someone would notice Kamal among the hordes is not surprising. His friends think of him as the friendliest person in all of Egypt. His smile shines a block away, and his large, green eyes are unforgettable. Joy radiates from every cell of his body, and he is immediately likable. Even when he was arrested for evangelizing Muslims and questioned for hours by the secret police, they ended the interrogation by telling him how glad they were he had stopped by for a visit!

Kamal loves Jesus with his whole heart and is a remarkable pray-er. It's an experience of heaven simply to be in the room when he prays. One man, upon hearing Kamal pray for the first time, was so overwhelmed by Kamal's passion for God that he sat speechless for several minutes after the prayer was over.

Kamal wants to be married, and he will tell anyone that. And one other personal characteristic also makes him stand out in a crowd: he's overweight, but he's "working on it." Still, none of these personal characteristics mattered the moment Noor, a committed Muslim mother of eight, spotted him in the Khan.

"Jesus walked with me alongside a lake, and He told me how much He loves me." The woman in black told Kamal details of the vivid dream she'd had the night before their meeting. "I think my husband loved me at one time. But that love I felt in my dream—His love—was different than anything I've ever experienced. I've never felt so much peace in my heart. I didn't want to leave. I didn't want Him to leave. I asked this Jesus, 'Why are You visiting me, a poor Muslim mother with eight children?' And all He said was, 'I love you, Noor. I have given everything for you. I died for you.'"

The din of the market faded from Kamal's consciousness. He heard only Noor describing her otherworldly encounter with Jesus Christ.

"As He turned to leave, the last thing Jesus said was, 'Ask My friend tomorrow about Me. He will tell you all you need in order to understand why I've visited you.' 'But, Jesus, who is Your friend?' I pleaded in my dream. 'Here is My friend.' Jesus pointed behind us. 'He has been walking with us the whole time we've been together.'"

Only partially veiled, Noor stared at Kamal as if she'd been looking for him her whole life. She continued, "Before He said that, I had not noticed you. But you were there—standing nearby through the whole dream. Even though you had walked with us around the lake, I hadn't seen anyone but Jesus. I thought I was alone with Him. His face was magnificent. I couldn't take my eyes off Him.

"Jesus did not tell me your name, but you were wearing the same clothes you have on right now, and your glasses . . . they're the same too. In my dream, your face radiated in a way that told me Jesus was, indeed, your friend. I knew I would not forget your smile."

Kamal led Noor out of the main crowd to the edge of the souk and a patch of grass under a lone tree. The two sat down before Kamal spoke.

"Noor, my name is Kamal, and I'm a Jesus follower. I have loved Him with an undivided heart for ten years now and am honored to have been in your dream."

Noor stared into Kamal's green eyes, enthralled with the man's words.

"Jesus is touching the hearts of Muslims all over the world. He's calling them to salvation—real salvation—one at a time, by visiting them in dreams and visions." Kamal paused, thinking. "Is this your first dream about Jesus?"

Noor answered, hope in her eyes. "Yes, it's my first. Will I have more dreams?"

Kamal measured his answer. "You might have many dreams about Jesus. It depends on what He plans for you. It could be that one dream is all you need." Kamal wondered briefly just what his Lord had in mind for this woman. "You must have many questions."

"About a thousand," Noor blurted.

"Is this a safe place to talk?"

Noor understood the question behind the question. "My husband is at work, and besides, he lost interest in me long ago. I'm his third wife, and last year he took a fourth. She is very young, and her smooth skin, beautiful face, and shapely silhouette are all he

can think about. I barely see him. He won't come looking for me."
Anguish flickered across her face, but wonder quickly returned.
"We are safe here. Tell me about Jesus!"

Kamal spoke slowly. "He is calling you, Noor. He doesn't make
random visits. Your dream has a purpose that will transform you
on the inside." Kamal watched Noor to make sure she understood.
"Jesus wants you to be one of His followers. You've been privi-
leged to have a personal visit from Jesus Christ. You are chosen,
Noor. Even before you were born, Jesus planned this encounter
with you." Kamal looked away, into the mass of people surrounding them, then back at Noor. "He has not yet appeared to me like
this, but I pray that He does."

Noor felt authority she could trust in Kamal's voice. She sighed
deeply and put words to her first question: "Why would a prophet
say that He died for me? I have believed in Him, and we Muslims
respect Him." Noor stared past Kamal, slowly shaking her head.
"But He is much more than I thought He was. I have never been
loved like I was when Jesus walked with me in that dream. I felt no
fear." She looked again at Kamal. "For the first time in my life, I
felt no shame." Her voice dropped to a whisper; Kamal strained to
hear her. "Even though He's a man, I wasn't intimidated. I didn't
feel threatened. I felt . . . perfect peace." Noor smiled.

Kamal feared that discussing Islam could drive Noor away, but
he boldly turned the conversation in that direction. "That's what
He wants to give you, Noor. Before He went to the cross, Jesus
said, 'Peace I leave with you, My peace I give to you' (John 14:27
NKJV). You will not—cannot—find peace like that with anyone
else. No one but Jesus even has it to offer."

Kamal continued, "Noor, you've spent your life searching for

God through religion. I did the same thing. My religion was different than yours, but in the end, all religions amount to the same thing: frustration. They're filled with man-made rules that will supposedly get you to God. But the fact is, they don't."

Kamal could see in her eyes that Noor grasped this painful truth.

"Do you ever feel frustrated like that, Noor?"

"Yes. Yes, I do. Every day."

"Noor, have you ever watched people after daily prayers?" Kamal asked, not waiting for an answer. "I've sat outside the Al-Azhar Mosque on Friday as the 'faithful' come out from noon prayers. They never look very happy—or fulfilled. They don't have the kind of peace I see all over your face right now. Religion can't give you that. Your religion can't give you that." He let the words sink in.

Noor bristled. She studied Kamal's face, her teeth lightly clenched. She glanced at the ground and then eyed Kamal solemnly. "Are you asking me . . . to leave Islam?"

Kamal had stepped into the mine field. "I'm not asking you to do anything, Noor. But Jesus is asking you to follow Him." The sincerity in his deep, jade eyes validated his words. "Do you believe your dream was real?"

Noor's shoulders dropped as calm settled over her black form. She gazed at the ground. "I know it was real. It has shaken me to my core. I must find out all about Him."

"Then I will do my best to answer every question you have."

Three hours later, questions and answers still flowed between Kamal and Noor on their grass island. Finally, Noor threw back her head and exhaled deeply, pleased with their progress but exhausted from the influx of strange, new information.

"What do I do with all I've learned today? When I give my life to Jesus and I'm new on the inside, will I still be a Muslim?"

Kamal didn't answer.

Suddenly, Noor sat up straight. The energy of resolve rose in her voice. "I'm ready now. I want to follow Jesus."

"Are you willing to be persecuted for Jesus?" Kamal surprised himself with the question.

Noor sat silently.

Kamal's next question was even more unexpected. "Are you willing to die for Him?"

Noor seemed less shocked by the question than Kamal. "Is that what He's calling me to do?" she asked as matter-of-factly as if she wondered whether Jesus might want her to buy grapes at the market.

Now Kamal stared through the Friday crowd, wondering again what this brave woman's future may hold. "It could well be your fate, Noor. Jesus told His followers on the night He was arrested that there would be harsh persecutions for those who follow Him." He returned his focus to Noor. "It's our privilege to suffer like He did. He warned that 'the time is coming when anyone who kills you will think they are offering a service to God' (John 16:2)."

Noor sighed. "Jesus was talking about Islam. He had to be. That's what happens to Muslims who convert." Noor folded her hands and pressed them to the ground. "I should tell you something, Kamal. I saw a television program a month ago. Father Zakaria was talking about Jesus, and a few people called in to the program to debate him. He handled them with ease. I was amazed, though, because most of the people told him how Jesus had changed their lives. I could not believe my ears. These were Muslims! I remember thinking that they would probably die because of leaving Islam. Their families would see to that. You know all about honor killing, I presume?"

They looked at each other for several seconds in silence.

Noor nodded slightly in recognition of a new thought. "Jesus knew this was coming, didn't He?"

"I think He did," Kamal responded soberly.

Noor sucked in her breath, exhaled, and watched a shopper brush past. "Well, I'm not afraid. But . . . I have to think about this. I must go to the mosque or to some place private. I must pray. What about my children? It's all so new. I . . ."

Kamal smiled the same smile Noor had seen in her dream. "I understand. I will never forget this encounter, Noor. Neither should you. Jesus has made you a wonderful offer that you only have to accept. He is calling you. I will pray. Until we meet again."

The Land Where Dreams Come True

Noor's dream opened the door to her heart and mind and prepared her in this startling way to receive salvation one day. But something about Egypt and dreams seem to go together. The two have been connected since the first book of the Bible. Men of God in the Old Testament had dreams and visions. Isaiah's book was a vision. Daniel saw visions. So did Ezekiel. But so did Egyptian pagan kings.

Outside of the Scriptures, Egyptian history records a significant amount of information about dreams and visions, many of which became determining factors in the overall direction of the nation. Messages "from beyond" were so revered that they often played a decisive role in a pharaoh's national plans or governing policies.

Egyptian rulers regularly had their dreams analyzed when deciding whether to wage war or build a temple to a new god. Divine messages were considered accurate predictors of the future, and no dream was discounted. Scribes recorded dreams to support the pharaoh's actions at critical junctures in history.

One archaeological find close to the Pyramids revealed that an ancient Egyptian scribe named Kenhirkhopeshef kept a papyrus document called the *Dream Book*. The book is a catalog of 108 dreams and the activities and emotions that accompanied them. As evidenced by the variety of ancient Egyptian dialects used in the writing, this journal was handed down through the generations.

The *Dream Book* demonstrates highly subjective interpretations. Similar dreams that occurred at different times had widely differing interpretations. Some of the dreams addressed the struggles of everyday life, such as financial gain and loss, fasting, overeating, gossip, anger, drinking, pleasure, and ethics. One particularly fascinating aspect of the book is its division into two parts—"good dreams" and "bad dreams" (the bad dreams were written in red ink). Egyptians believed the gods could judge hearts and evaluate all human motives. Dreams and visions were one way in which the whims of the gods were revealed. Were the gods pleased or displeased with the Egyptians' efforts? What would be their ultimate fate in eternity? They were on the right theological track, but they had the wrong deity. Like no other nation, Egypt has been imprinted by dreams and visions.

Little wonder, then, that the God of Israel gave dreams to Pharaoh when Joseph was in an Egyptian prison. The ruler's troubling dreams set off alarms in the palace that wouldn't shut off until the king was certain of the interpretation. Priests, magicians, and wise men were at Pharaoh's disposal anytime a dream needed to be deciphered. But God spoke truth only through Joseph. All the other dream specialists were frauds, incapable of providing the correct interpretation to the king. It's no wonder Joseph made the quantum leap from prisoner to prime minister. From the days before his brothers sold him, Joseph had known the power, as well as the danger, of dreams.

EGYPTIAN DREAMS, UP CLOSE AND PERSONAL

Recently, my son John-Mark and I visited the Pyramids in Giza. These magnificent creations are just a short distance from Cairo, and if you survive the wild taxi ride there, you won't be disappointed. (A ride in an Egyptian taxi transforms you into a prayer warrior from the moment you leave the curb.)

The Sphinx, also located at Giza, was built around 2500 BC—about seven hundred years before Joseph came to Egypt and eleven hundred years before Moses' time. Although this curious creature with a human head and body of a lion is crumbling because of wind, humidity, and the smog from Cairo, it has managed to survive this long in part because it was buried in sand for almost one thousand years—until King Thutmose IV had a dream.

As a young prince in Egypt, Thutmose claimed that a god spoke to him in a dream at the Sphinx after he had spent the day hunting near there. Thutmose had fallen asleep beside the small portion of the creature that protruded above the sand at the time. The god Hamarkis told Thutmose to clear away the sand from the Sphinx since it was choking the creature. Hamarkis promised that if Thutmose was faithful to this task, he would be rewarded with a kingship. The young prince cleared away the sand and soon became king over Egypt.

King Thutmose IV was one of the most feared kings of the Eighteenth Dynasty and well known for his bloodthirsty reign. To commemorate his alleged dream and to add credibility to his kingship, Thutmose placed a stela (an inscribed stone marker) between the front paws of the Sphinx telling his story. The Dream Stela is still there today and in fairly good shape, considering that it is more than thirty-four hundred years old.

What's curious about this particular event is that no one could verify that this dream actually took place. The prince told the story, and it became the basis for his kingship. The only evidence was his unsubstantiated testimony.

With a history like this, people pay attention when dreams hit home. And Christ followers like Kamal are the new Josephs, placed there by God to interpret dreams. The need for explanation is so great, in fact, that this ad appeared recently in the *Cairo Times*: "Have you seen a man in a white robe in a dream? If so, call this number . . ."

Ah, the power of dreams in Egypt!

TWO

The Imam and the Gun

W ho would you guess is the toughest sort of Muslim to reach? A terrorist, perhaps? Anyone willing to blow himself up to kill "infidels" seems as committed to Islam as they come, right?

That would be a reasonable speculation, of course, but I know of former terrorists walking with Jesus now in every Middle Eastern country. We work with many of them to reach other Muslims with the gospel. This new breed of disciples has been changed radically for Christ. The presence of the Holy Spirit is so strong in their lives, you would never suspect their shady pasts when you first meet them. These former terrorists are "Exhibit A" when it comes to the transforming power of Christ.

Suicide bombers are tough, but as I see it, the hardest Muslims to reach are the imams. An imam is the leader of the local mosque. His job is to keep the Muslim flock in line with the Qur'an. These spiritual leaders are steeped in Islamic teaching and propaganda. As the guardians of Islam, imams live to defend their religion at all costs—usually the cost of the life of anyone who dares to convert to Christianity. So when someone shares Christ with them, imams are usually combative, angry, and arrogant. While a few have a softer demeanor, most retain the jagged personal edge necessary to coerce Muslims into submission on a daily basis.

Muslims usually fear the imams because of the enormous power they wield within the community. If they live in a country where Sharia Law has been adopted, then imams, along with the religious police, are the enforcers. When Muslims come to Christ, converts often liken imams to the religious leaders who threatened Jesus in the New Testament. Think *Pharisee with a Qur'an in his hand*, and you have the picture.

In Egypt, imams seem to be everywhere—and there's a good reason for that.

Egypt is the intellectual center of Islam. An imam who studies at Egypt's Al-Azhar University (just down the street from the marketplace where Kamal met Noor) is respected throughout the Islamic world. In many ways, Egypt, and specifically Cairo, is the hub of the religion. Al-Azhar was founded in AD 970 and claims to be the world's center for Arabic literature and Sunni Islamic learning. In Mecca and Medina, Saudi Arabia may have the two holiest sites of Islam, but Egypt shapes the religion. Saudi Arabia is the heart of Islam; Egypt is the brains. It makes a great place for Jesus to visit.

IMAM'S THE WORD

Hassan startled awake to a rough hand clamped firmly over his mouth. Heart racing, he felt the cold muzzle of a gun in his right temple.

"Don't say a word." A masked voice whispered the command in the dark. "Get up, and come with me."

For several minutes, Hassan rubbed sleep from his eyes as his kidnapper shoved him through the streets of Cairo's old city. Hassan had no doubt he had been discovered as one who leads Muslims to faith in Christ. Despite his best efforts to evangelize quietly, one convert at a time, Cairo had found him out. It is one of the riskiest places in the world for Muslim evangelism.

Hassan had moved to this section of Old Cairo two years earlier. Gifted at bringing Jesus into conversations with Muslim friends, he had yet to see anyone in this neighborhood become a Christ follower. But he had tried daily.

Stumbling through one quiet block after another with a gun to his back, Hassan cried out to God, *Isn't anyone awake to help me?* But two hours before the morning call to prayer, Cairo still slept. Not that anyone would care, of course. An imam pushing a Christian through this place wouldn't garner any sympathy for the victim. They would assume—as Hassan did just now—that he was on his way to a well-deserved execution.

The rough grip on Hassan's right arm shoved him along quickly, jerking him intermittently for course corrections deemed necessary by his captor. As his death march progressed, Hassan's thoughts drifted to his rapidly concluding mission here in Egypt. He had studied Islam for years—learning the Qur'an, the Hadith (sayings of Muhammad compiled several centuries after his death), and the teachings of most leading Islamic scholars—all for the purpose of knowing the beliefs of Muslims whom he hoped God would transform into brothers and sisters in Christ. The Lord had birthed a passion in Hassan to reach Muslims, but all of his preparation didn't matter, it seemed, on his way to becoming another Egyptian martyr.

"Up the stairs." The harsh voice interrupted Hassan's musings.

Hassan wondered how his secret had been revealed, and by whom.

Blood pounded in his veins from fear and the exertion of a five-story climb up the back steps of an aging building with his captor.

"We have to jump off this building onto the roof of that one over there. It's the only way to get in."

For the first time since leaving his apartment, Hassan looked squarely at his abductor's face. Only then did he realize the man had blackened his face to obscure his features. Hassan glanced into the gaping space at which the man now pointed his gun and then stared back at the intense eyes gleaming from the dark visage.

"There's no way I can jump from this building to that one!" Hassan blurted.

"You can, and you will. Get a running start." His captor pointed the muzzle at Hassan. "You go first."

Whether death would come from a bullet or a fall to the pavement fifty feet below, Hassan didn't know, but he believed his companion would use his weapon with the slightest provocation. At least the jump—even if it failed—would extend his life a few more seconds. And if he made it across the gap, who knows what might yet save him?

Adrenaline—and angels, perhaps—yielded the most magnificent leap of Hassan's life. He landed with room to spare, and his obviously practiced kidnapper thumped beside him, pistol still in hand, two seconds later.

The assailant seized Hassan's right arm again and forced him toward a hatchway in the abandoned warehouse. Hassan was sure he would never again see the night sky. He whispered, "Jesus, into Your hands I commit my spirit."

The man flinched almost imperceptibly at Hassan's prayer. Hassan noticed the fleeting cut of the man's eyes toward him. The grip on Hassan's arm tightened.

"Open the hatch door, and climb in quickly." The gun again pointed the way.

Hassan saw himself struggle through the opening as if he were an actor in a movie thriller. He hoped the scene wouldn't end too quickly, and once inside the gloomy structure, the plot took a startling twist. He recounts what happened over the next several incredible minutes.

"I stepped into a foreboding room, lit with a single candle, fully expecting my immediate execution. Ten obviously Muslim men stood in a circle and stared at me as I entered. They ordered me to sit down. When I complied, the menacing atmosphere changed instantly. The mysterious group smiled at me."

The man who had kidnapped Hassan spoke first. "We are imams, and we all studied at Al-Azhar University. During our time there, each of us had a dream about Jesus, and each of us has privately become a follower of Christ. For a time, we didn't dare tell anyone about this. It would, of course, have been our own death sentences. But finally, we could hide it no longer.

"We each prayed to Jesus for His help to learn what it means to be His follower. Over time, He brought us together, and you can imagine our amazement when the Holy Spirit revealed that there are other imams who have found Jesus as well. Now we meet here three times a week at night to pray for our families and for the people in our mosques to find Jesus too. We know you follow Christ. He led us to you."

Hassan recalls, "I was speechless. Then I was so relieved, I laughed for several minutes while the group watched."

The kidnapper finally explained the point of this clandestine encounter. "I'm very sorry I had to frighten you with the mask and the gun, but I knew it was the only way to get you here. It was just too dangerous any other way. I apologize. But now our question is, will you teach us the Bible?"

PART · II

SAUDI ARABIA—THE FORBIDDEN NATION

THREE

Infidel Gathering

A bu Badr has an unusual job. He decapitates people for a living. Stranger still, his work is the family business. Abu's father was an executioner, and neither of them had to submit a résumé to get the job. The government of Saudi Arabia appointed each in his time as chief executioner for the city of Mecca. Whether Badr will pass the mantle to his son remains to be seen because for now, Abu's career is, so to speak, still in full swing.

"Everyone is a bit worried when he starts a new job and is afraid he will fail," Badr once explained in a television interview. "But I quickly got used to it. Along with the hundreds of beheadings I've handled, I carry out the punishment of cutting off thieves' hands, as well as the cutting off of a hand and a leg on alternate sides, as instructed in the Qur'an. I have beheaded many people who were my friends, but anyone who commits an offense brings it on himself."

The interviewer asked if Badr ever had to kill more than one person at a time, to which the executioner replied coolly, "Allah be praised, there is nothing to it. Three, four, five, or six—it doesn't matter. It's entirely normal. An execution is an execution." Badr chuckled. "As long as the person stands straight, it makes our job much easier."

In Saudi Arabia, an executioner is something of a celebrity. There are only six official executioners in the country. And among them, Abu Badr is the most prestigious. He metes out Qur'anic justice at Islam's holiest site, the religion's epicenter: Mecca.

MISERY-LOVING COMPANY

Several million Muslim faithful flood Saudi Arabia during the hajj, the monthlong annual pilgrimage to Mecca, and it seemed to Amir Issak that all of them were crammed in the passport line in front of him. *What must the crowds be like at the Kaaba stone itself?* He shuddered at the image of Ramadan hordes gathering at Mecca's holiest of sites and breathed a prayer of thanks to no one in particular that he wouldn't be among them. Once through the endless passport line, Amir wouldn't go anywhere near Mecca. Besides knowing that as an "infidel" (non-Muslim), he would be a dead man for even attempting a visit there, nothing in his spirit—if there was such a thing—cared in the slightest for that sort of meaninglessness. His visit to Muhammad's home country was strictly for business.

Does anyone in this country ever smile? Amir pondered the glumness he saw in the faces around him as the masses bustled toward what would be a once-in-a-lifetime spiritual experience for most of them. He laughed to himself but felt like shouting, "This airport is a joke—and so is your magical hajj!"

"Religion melts the intellect," he muttered under his breath, shifting the weight of the suit bag slung over his right shoulder. *These people are lifeless robots—filled with nothing but an obsession over their duty to Allah.* Only the rich financial rewards he gained from trips to Saudi Arabia gave him the resolve to put up with what he told his friends was "religious lunacy."

Amir enjoyed his coworkers' nickname for him: "the party guy." Being born a Christian—after all, that's what one was in Jordan if not a Muslim—was only a little better than being a Muslim in Amir's estimation. But at least his family didn't have to endure the pilgrimage compulsion. His religion left him alone to do pretty much as he pleased, and making as much money as possible was what pleased Amir. Why his employer, the Jordanian Office of Tourism, had insisted he take the trip south across the border this week of all weeks was still not clear to him, but he would make the most of meetings with his contacts in the Saudi government. He'd now tolerated enough crooked deals with Muslims to put his distrust of Islamic businessmen to work in his own favor. Yet it merely bolstered his revulsion at the Muhammadans.

As the line of travelers seeped through the passport checkpoint, Amir stared curiously at a man nearing the exit. He reminded Amir of Jamal Hussein. He and Jamal had spent countless hours during their years of friendship analyzing a mutual distaste for Islam. He replayed in his mind a conversation last week at Via Seven, their favorite, out of the way bar in Amman.

"I suppose I'm the real fool for staying here." Amir sipped his second Amstel Light. He wrapped both hands around the moist glass and touched his lower lip to the rim. "If I wanted to be free of anything to do with Islam, I should be traveling more in the United States, or at least Europe."

"Well, the next time you visit your relatives in San Jose, why don't you ask to rent their spare room?" Jamal chuckled at the comment, knowing Amir would never sacrifice his independence by living in someone else's house.

Amir glanced sideways, nodding at his friend's jest. "You think I wouldn't be happy in California? I know I complain about too many Muslims moving to America, but at least their women aren't yet wrapped in tent cloth. I prefer the virgins I can look at to the ones only imagined in the future." Amir paused, enjoying that thought before his lip curled at the next. "If I never heard a call to prayer again for the rest of my life, I would be happy."

Jamal smiled. "You think leaving the Middle East would be the greatest reward for your hard work? No, I think you enjoy your disdain for Islam too much. Besides, you would be boring to talk with if you had no mosques, no calls to prayer, no burkas, and no imams calling people to jihad to whine about. I believe you enjoy the adventure of knowing your opinions could get you killed too much."

"At least those who would kill me wouldn't be anyone I care about. You, on the other hand, would be the victim of your own family if they knew your real views. Your royal cousin would have turned his pet lions loose on you." Amir loved to remind Jamal of his apostasy.

Jamal's family were committed Muslims, deeply rooted in the short history of Jordan and distantly related to the country's late king. Government, business, religion, education, and other noble endeavors consumed the Hussein family, but Jamal cared no more about Islam than Amir. Educated in the best religious schools in the Middle East, Jamal had studied the Qur'an since he could read.

It was, in fact, the first—and for a long time, only—thing he was *allowed* to read. But Jamal lost his religion one year at the hajj.

One evening together, Amir and Jamal had watched the Al-Jazeera interview with chief executioner Abu Badr without moving or speaking. Finally Amir broke the silence. "That man is sick! See, Jamal, that is the problem with Islam. It hasn't progressed for fourteen centuries. It's in a permanent time warp. How can this butcher slaughter people each day and then go home and have dinner with his family? Has his conscience evaporated? And yet he's some perverse kind of celebrity in Mecca. The sword of Islam that he swings every day is on the Saudi flag. That says it all."

"You know, Amir, you don't have to convince me. When I made the hajj to Mecca, I saw Abu Badr at work. And that was the end of the religion for me."

In addition to the heartless executions, Jamal had seen through the spiritual obsessions to the real substance of the Muslim holy city, no different than the worst of secular humanity. Money and power drove Mecca. Hotel prices skyrocket for the hajj, just in time for pilgrims to arrive. Outside the pricier lodgings, conditions are filthier than the people who jam the city. And even though he never shared his true thoughts with his family, Jamal believed he could see flickers of doubt even in the eyes of his parents. They had done their best to make him proud of his Hashemite bloodline, but the undeniable realities he saw around him—and eventually the influence of his best friend—overmatched his parents' diligent training. A common hatred of Islam sealed the relationship between Jamal and Amir.

"But I do have the right papers!" A man's rage cut through Amir's thoughts. A passport inspector, now just four people away from Amir, had denied entry to an elderly Iranian. "You are making an issue just because I'm Shia," he screamed. The man glanced self-righteously at nearby witnesses who stared blankly back at the offender.

"You don't have the correct identification, so you are being sent back to Tehran on the next flight!"

Amir expected to see a fistfight break out right in front of him like the one last year. *That man was Iranian, too*, he noted, his thoughts drifting back to Jamal's satirical commentary on the hajj and the revered city itself.

"Who but Muslims would want Mecca, anyway? It's a pile of sand with a puny black rock in the middle of it. I can't believe so many people waste a life's savings just to go pray there." Jamal had looked solemnly at Amir, mocking his own words. "Perhaps that's one real difference between Muslims and Christians. Christians have better taste in vacation destinations."

"What a great theologian you are." Amir smiled at his friend's treatise. "*If* there's a difference, that's the only one. Both religions have come and gone. Go to a mosque. Go to a church. Either place, there's nothing but a bunch of old people inside. People who pay attention to real life have better things to do with their time. I know I do."

An irritated hand motioned for Amir's passport. He hadn't noticed how quickly the Syrian in front of him had moved through the checkpoint. Shouts from the Iranian Shiite being forced back through the terminal faded into the drone of the crowd as the border official glanced at Amir's travel documents. The slap of a stamp on paper was the signal that his mission for the God he disdained was about to begin.

The Accidental Pilgrim

Chaos at the terminal had spilled into the streets of Riyadh and followed Amir all the way to the Intercontinental Hotel, but three hours by a swimming pool at the five-star haven diluted the stress of Amir's airport experience and his hair-raising cab ride south into the city. His conversation in the taxi with another businessman from Jordan had helped make the trip bearable. Amir appreciated the serendipity that Ziad was an acquaintance of Amir's cousin in Amman. Both men lamented the bad timing of their respective visits to the Saudi peninsula but exchanged business cards in hopes that their chance meeting would at some point substantiate the value of having endured the hajj.

As Amir roused himself from the poolside chair to return to his room, his cell phone bleeped Cousin Sahar's ringtone.

"Greetings, my cousin."

"And greetings to you, my ever-wandering relative. You left me a message."

Amir had been glad for the excuse to call Sahar. The two always enjoyed talking together, but neither busy man ever called the other without a specific reason. This time it was Amir's encounter with Ziad. "There are two million visitors passing through Riyadh, and I happened into a taxi with someone you know."

Sahar laughed in response.

"Ziad Something. I don't recall his last name."

"Oh, yes. He's in the travel business, like you. I don't know him well, but he seems likeable. And you know what? I can't remember his last name either. Now I'll be embarrassed when I see him again."

"Well, cousin, I can save you some shame. He gave me his card. I'll check it when I get back to my room and let you know."

Sahar was as nominally Christian as Amir and moaned sympathetically through the traveler's account of arriving in the Saudi capital during hajj. They agreed to sit together over a beer as soon as life settled down. Their phone call lasted through the lobby. Amir tapped the off spot on his phone and jabbed the elevator call button.

Once in his room, Amir emptied every pocket in the case of his MacBook Pro, searching for Ziad's business card. Amir's passport dropped onto the bed. Then he remembered. He had taken his passport from the inside pocket of his sport coat, slipped his new friend's card between the pages, and stuffed the passport into his computer case.

Amir flipped to the business card, but before his brain could register Ziad's last name, a shocking entry on page twenty-two caught his attention. "Muslim" was stamped across his identity. The passport checker's error was unfathomable. Only Muslims were allowed entry into the sacred cities, and misidentifying a visitor during the hajj likely carried a cruel penalty for the erring official if discovered. Amir was also disgusted at the thought of being classified among the religious nuts.

"Muslim!" Amir said aloud to the empty hotel room. "How could they think I was a Muslim?"

But the answer was obvious. A low-paid government employee who was verbally assaulted moments earlier and distracted by agitated hordes could easily make the assumption that anyone looking like a Middle Easterner in Saudi Arabia during the hajj would be Muslim. Still, in all of his travels, Amir had never heard of *this* happening. And as far as governing authorities are concerned, "once a

Muslim, always a Muslim." It would take an act of the Jordanian Parliament to get the stamp removed. For purposes of international travel, Amir was now a Muslim.

Dinner at the hotel restaurant met Amir's high expectations. With that and several hours of pay-per-view, the passport oversight wandered from his mind. Amir flicked off the light and faded to sleep on top of the quilted bedspread.

Whether hours or minutes later, Amir couldn't tell, but he awoke startled, his breathing stopped. He had heard a voice in the dark. Amir lay petrified, listening to the room in which *he* should have been the only presence.

"Pray for them." The voice came again, strong and authoritative.

Amir bolted upright and swung his feet to the floor. His pulse surged as if he'd just gulped three cups of Turkish coffee, but in the same instant, all fear washed from his body. A magnificent calm engulfed him.

"Pray for them." At the words, Amir's room exploded in light. A majestic, manlike being stepped from nowhere into the room. The angel stood serenely at the foot of the bed, his sense of purpose obvious.

"You have a mission, Amir."

Amir gaped, not in fear, but in wonder at the power and peace in the visitor's voice.

"Go, and pray for them in Mecca. Be faithful, Amir."

The messenger's eyes rested for an instant on Amir's before the creature disappeared, taking the light with him. The encounter had lasted mere seconds, but the change Amir already sensed in his heart felt like wisdom that could only have accumulated over decades. He sat alone on his bed and stared at the dark.

The next day, Amir drifted through the motions of business, his mind on the previous night's unexpected guest. He nibbled at lunch and spent the afternoon . . . praying. When had he done that before? He wasn't sure all that he said made sense, but even the rote prayers he conjured from distant memory seemed full of a reality he'd never known before. Yesterday's passion for the travel industry had been replaced by a longing for his—the angel had given him the word—*mission*.

From Sarcasm to Compassion

When commitments forced him into meetings, Amir said almost nothing. Several times, an associate asked what he was looking at as Amir gazed out the window. He didn't see the buildings of Riyadh. His stare took him beyond, to his mind's-eye view of Muslims swarming Mecca. The longer he gazed, the more love for these people he had derided just days ago flowed into his soul. He struggled to identify this visceral feeling more clearly. Slowly he recognized that he was feeling tenderness. Tenderness toward people as harsh as most Muslims made no sense to him. Yet he was irresistibly consumed by compassion for them.

His work in Riyadh concluded at last with a seminar conducted by Arab World Travel. As the presenter offered his formal thanks to the participants, Amir flipped open his laptop, clicked to the airline's website, and changed his reservation for the flight home to five days later.

That night, Amir surfed online to an Arabic Bible and began reading the New Testament. When he finished the book of Matthew, he closed his computer and turned off the light.

"Follow Me, Amir." A voice and the same penetrating light awakened Amir again. This time, the figure wasn't an angel. The instant Amir opened his eyes, he knew the Person standing in his room was Jesus. "Come to Me and receive the Gift."

And as before, the room went just as quickly dark. Alone, Amir flicked on the bedside light and grabbed his laptop. He opened the Bible he had downloaded that evening and searched for the words "Follow Me." He chose a familiar reference in Matthew 9:9.

I am Matthew in the story, Amir observed. A hated tax collector, Matthew had received grace and left everything to follow Jesus. He never returned to his previous life, but he knew he was forgiven. Amir realized, *Jesus has reached out to me in spite of my sinful, sarcastic emptiness.*

The stories of Jesus that Amir had listened to as a child replayed in his mind. He remembered how, as a boy, he had loved Jesus. Formal Christianity eventually erased all traces of that affection, but now it rushed into his soul.

Amir tossed the computer on to a pillow and slipped off the bed to his knees: "Lord Jesus, I have been so far from You. I've even hated You. Please forgive me. Forgive my sin-infested life. You died for me just like You did for Matthew. I repent. I'm Yours, Lord. I'll follow You anywhere."

Appointment with a Sword

Yes, thought Amir, if people see me, they will have no trouble believing I'm a Muslim. Amir chuckled softly at his image in the mirror at Haddad Brothers clothing store. He had never worn the traditional Muslim robe. Only his shoes peered from beneath the hem of the unadorned, white dishdasha. A complexly woven red-and-white kaffiyeh framed his face.

His shopping complete, Amir grabbed a taxi to Riyadh's bus station and arrived just in time for the 10 a.m. bus to Mecca. He was astounded but relieved that there was room for him onboard.

The four-hundred-mile trip passed quickly. Amir was lost in his new experience of inner peace. He had never felt so close to Jesus. As the miles sped past the bus window, Amir prayed. He prayed for his own commitment to be faithful as both the angel and Jesus had charged him. He prayed for his family, for Jamal—how would he explain this to *him*?—and for his cousin Sahar. He prayed for the Muslims around him. He prayed for Mecca.

In the fading evening light, the flash of a sign in the bus head-lights interrupted Amir's new prayer life: "Non-Muslims who enter this city will be killed." It was the final warning to unwelcome visitors.

I'll never get out of here alive. It was a thought, not a prayer. *There are so many watching for infiltrators and religious violations at every site. Sharia is the law here.* Amir remembered Abu Badr's manic chuckle over the assignment of beheading several people in one execution session. He replayed in his mind Jamal's description of the killings he had witnessed: "One by one they were pronounced apostate. In seconds—with no hope of appeal and certainly no mercy—Badr severed the victim's head, and a team of assistants tossed two lifeless body parts in a pile." Jamal said he had vomited after the third execution.

With that thought, Amir grasped at his chest. Feeling only the dishdasha, he breathed a sigh of relief. Thankfully, he had remembered to leave his cross necklace at the hotel in Riyadh. How ironic it would have been to lose his head for wearing a symbol that for years had hung meaninglessly around his neck.

The bus stopped within sight of the Sacred Mosque, and with surprising calm, Amir thought, *So this is where I die.*

COMPASSIONATE VIGIL

Well rested from the previous day's bus ride, Amir joined the faithful hordes at the Kaaba stone. As the human mass shuffled counterclockwise around the holy relic, Amir could not believe he was in the middle of it all.

What Amir had scorned as madness of the hajj less than a week ago now filled him with compassion. *Jesus faced crowds,* Amir reflected on his reading of Matthew, *and He felt this too.* His thoughts were strange to him, but he wanted to touch every person thronging the Sacred Mosque. *I don't hate them anymore.* Instead, the deep love he now felt for Jesus spilled into his attitude toward these desperate pilgrims. Bible stories he had heard in his childhood surfaced in his mind with new meaning. *God sent the prophet Jonah on a mission. Did Jonah hate the people as I have hated Muslims, or did God change his heart too?*

Soaring desert temperatures and the press of so many people created a stifling heat. Amir struggled to breathe, but trying to exit against the crowd was impossible. He would not be able to leave until this throng completed its seventh lap around the ancient meteorite.

To distract himself from the agony, Amir turned his attention to the people crushing one another around him. Some were crying.

Others were emotionless, like robots obeying their programming. *No wonder people are trampled here*, thought Amir. The flow could not stop even if someone tripped and fell. But still, desperate faces regurgitated their prayers while bodies hung on one another in a life-or-death march. Amir's heart broke to see so many well-intentioned souls torturing themselves to placate a false god. All came in search of a blessing from Allah, and all left still searching.

SINISTER VISITATION

Amir smelled the cigarette smoke as he unlocked the door to his hotel room. He peered in to see his clothes scattered across the bed and his suitcase open upside-down on the floor. His laptop no longer lay on the easy chair where he had left it but now sat on the desk.

"Secret police." Amir said the words aloud to the disheveled room. He batted at smoke still swirling from cigarettes that had obviously been in the room just moments before he had entered. Amir closed his eyes and rubbed his forehead with his right hand. "I'm being watched," he murmured. "How have I given myself away? Is my room is bugged?"

It had been only thirty minutes since he left the Sacred Mosque. The taxi he shared with an arguing husband and wife had dropped the couple first at the Grand Zamzam and then proceeded to Amir's hotel, the Nawazi Aziziah. Amir's stomach churned as he recalled the chaotic ride and the one crucial fact he hadn't noticed on the way here: he had never told the taxi driver where to go!

He was one of them. Amir could hardly believe his own obvious conclusion. How the word to check out Amir had passed so quickly he couldn't fathom, but it was clear now that he must not give anyone he encountered a reason to question his motives for being in Mecca.

Amir removed the SIM card from his iPhone, dropped it into a dirty sock, and stashed the potentially incriminating information in a side pocket of his suitcase. He slid the cell phone battery into the case for his glasses and tucked that into his leather shoulder bag. No phone calls, no computer contact from now on. He had company.

Become as a Muslim to Win a Muslim

The next morning, Amir awoke to a renewed sense of boldness for his mission. The dread he felt in the aftermath of the secret police intrusion had left him. His confidence returned, and he even smiled as he asked himself, What did I expect? I'm in Mecca.

This time, Amir joined pilgrims in the smaller city of Mina just outside of Mecca for their ritual stoning of the devil. Muslim faithful gather at the town's Jamarat walls to take aim at Satan and his minions. This particular hajj duty requires the follower of Allah to throw stones accurately enough to strike the walls forty-nine times during a three-day stint. (Until 2004, three Jamarat pillars were the targets, but hurling rocks through crowds at the much-harder-to-hit goals caused significant injuries to those gathered around.)

Amir watched silently, amazed by the collective display of

anger. Men and women screamed as they hurled stones at an imaginary devil. Unlike any religious ceremony he had ever witnessed, the seething hatred seemed barely contained, as if the swarm would erupt at any moment and destroy each other in the name of vanquishing the devil. It reminded Amir of a protest in Amman that had exploded into a deadly riot the year before.

Lost in his observations, Amir wasn't sure how long the two men had been watching him. They stood at the edge of the crowd, their eyes fixed on Amir. Both wore white dishdashas with red-and-white kaffiyehs. The face of the notably tall one featured the footlong beard of a Muslim cleric while his foil was overtly short and fat.

Amir slithered into the crowd for cover and picked up a handful of stones. Soon he was lost in the multitude, hurling rocks and shrieking at the walls. His mind raced, *What am I doing to cause suspicion? Do they know about my passport? Is it the way I pray?* He arrived at no satisfactory answers for himself, but at least when he surfaced thirty minutes later at the spot where he had entered the mob, the men were gone.

On the last day of the hajj, during Eid-al-Adha, which honors Abraham's willingness to sacrifice Ishmael (not Isaac, according to Islamic tradition), Amir's soul wept at the sight of the mass animal sacrifice. He cried to the real God of Abraham to set these people free from their torturous existence.

It was also the day Amir finally saw him—Abu Badr. He flinched as he watched Abu Badr raise his Jowhar and amputate another head at the King Abdul Aziz Gate. One execution was enough, and Amir turned away, yet not in fear. He had never, in fact, felt less fear. Now a dedicated and determined follower of

Christ, Amir thought of nothing but his newfound love for the Muslims.

Amir thanked Jesus for filling his heart with love for these people and for calling him to this strategic mission. His prayer assignment moved him from the masses surrounding the Kaaba east to Muhammad's Mount Arafat. There, glued to his position overlooking the city, he prayed for the pilgrims and against their unearthly oppressors. Amir could not remember where he had heard the term, but he identified the conflict as spiritual warfare.

After several hours, the emotional strain of his five days in Mecca combined with the exertion of his prayer rendered him exhausted. As he was about to relent and return to his hotel to rest for the trip home, he overheard two sentences of a conversation that electrified him.

"It is my third dream about Jesus since I have been here." The pair of men passing Amir were obviously trusted friends. The man who had spoken eyed the ground ahead of him and continued without looking at his companion. "But what does it mean?"

Amir wanted to shout of his own experience to these men before they dissolved into the crowd, but he was not here for that. Instead, the comments so reenergized his spirit that he wandered, praying, around the sacred mountain for the rest the afternoon.

When he finally felt as if his work for the day was done, Amir turned toward his hotel. Walking across the plaza at the base of the craggy hill, a man joined him stride for stride. The stranger said nothing and looked straight ahead. Uneasy with the odd encounter, Amir veered away from the man. This was certainly it. The stranger would undoubtedly shadow him from a distance, and at some point between here and his hotel, secret police would materialize from the crowd, and Amir would disappear. *Abu Badr awaits me.*

Despite instincts telling him he shouldn't, Amir glanced over his right shoulder. The breath caught in his throat when he saw the man just three paces behind him. After Amir had turned, the pursuer waited just long enough to avoid being seen by Amir before approaching again. Amir sickened as the man smiled—or was it a smirk? Both men stopped and for several tense seconds eyed one another before the stranger's grin softened.

"I am your friend," he said. "My name is Muhammad."

Muhammad turned and dissolved into the sea of pilgrims.

Busted?

Throughout the night, Amir brooded over the encounter with Muhammad. Just what kind of a "friend" was he, really? Amir wanted to believe the man meant well, but doubts remained as he checked out of his hotel the next morning. After signing the bill, he turned from the service desk and paused to scan faces in the lobby. Would he see the two men who had stalked him yesterday in Mina? Or would Muhammad be there with a crew of police thugs? Seeing no one suspicious set his mind only slightly more at ease. They'll wait for me to leave the hotel. Then I'll be arrested. The smoke was so thick again in my room last night when I walked in; they can't be ignoring me.

Only then did the gloom of his thoughts strike him as odd. He had survived five anxious days of hajj in the city most lethal to infidels, and in a few hours he would be safely out of reach of the

Meccan authorities. God had protected him this long, and there was no reason to think His mercy would abandon Amir now.

He walked the few blocks to Mecca's bus station, paid the fare to Riyadh, and settled into a back-row seat. He buried himself in a newspaper he had picked up off the bus station floor.

At the first stop, Amir dropped the newspaper below eye level so he could see the commotion that had flared at the front of the bus. Two secret police were yelling at the driver and holding a photograph in front on his face. The driver shook his head, and the goon clutching the picture motioned for the bus to continue. As the bus accelerated, the two officials began slowly down the center aisle, scrutinizing the passport of each passenger and comparing it with the photo the men had brought with them.

Amir watched the ominous progress in his direction for a dozen excruciating minutes. The official who had yelled at the driver had started through the bus before his companion and was halfway down the aisle when the bus arrived at its next destination. The man stumbled backward at the final jolt as the bus stopped. Regaining his footing, he turned and screamed at the driver to keep the back door closed, but it was too late for the driver's practiced hand.

As the door gaped, Amir sprang up and scuttled past the two rows between his seat and the blessed opening. Before the driver could respond to the command, Amir rolled down the steps and slammed onto the pavement. The pain of his rude contact with the ground had not even fully registered in Amir's consciousness before the door slammed shut and the bus roared off. Amir cowered on the sidewalk by a parked car and prayed for a taxi. His heart sank as the bus stopped thirty feet away, and the front door swung open. The passport checkers leaped to the curb, scanning the scene.

Preoccupied with his pursuers, Amir didn't hear the car pull up beside him, but a voice cut into his thoughts.

"Hey, friend, it's Muhammad. Do you need a ride?"

He looked in the direction of the words, and as the back car door opened, he saw the same smile he'd seen the day before. Amir scrambled into the taxi and lay on the floor in the backseat as it slipped past the bus.

"Is everything okay, brother?"

Amir pulled himself up and looked at Muhammad, who had scrunched into the corner of the seat to make room for the prone Amir.

"Brother?" Amir whispered the question.

The Islamic call to prayer playing on the cab's radio covered Muhammad's response, keeping it between the two men in the backseat.

"Yes, brother. You are not alone here. When I came to Mecca on the hajj a few years ago, Jesus appeared to me." He let the statement sink in with Amir. "I began to seek Him, and now I am a follower. I never thought I would come back to Mecca. But He has called me—us. There are others. Many were led here, just like you." Muhammad stared into Amir's eyes. "'Pray for them' is all He told us."

Amir's gaze drifted from Muhammad's face. His head drooped to the seat, and his eyes closed in a wordless prayer of thanks as the car sped away from Mecca.

Jesus Sightings in Mecca

Worldwide, Christians are being martyred in greater numbers today than any other time in the last twenty centuries of

Christianity, and Muslim nations usually dominate Voice of the Martyrs' annual "Most Dangerous Countries" list.[1] These nations often claim officially that everyone has the right to practice his or her own religion in their country. But the unspoken rule is that freedom of religion does not include Muslims who want to become followers of Jesus. Conversion erases all pretense of religious freedom.

Because 1.5 billion Muslims look to Saudi Arabia as home base for their faith, Saudi Arabia rises to the top when it comes to "zero tolerance" toward other religions. The House of Saud has decreed that persecution and death are to be expected by anyone who attempts to part ways with "the religion of the sword." Despite the various interpretations of the Qur'an, warring sects, and international religious wars, this Muslim kingdom is the unifying force within Islam. And like an ancient fortress city, the birthplace of Muhammad and spiritual capital of Mecca remains for Muslims the most controlled and revered spot on the planet. For centuries, Mecca has been 100 percent Muslim. Medina, where Muhammad died at age sixty-two, is similarly honored and is as hostile to outsiders as Mecca. Yet in both places, Jesus is at work.

Hajj pilgrims like Amir and Muhammad continue to report new phenomena. One leader in Jordan recounts that a man sought him out after making the hajj. His friend told him, "I went to the hajj to get close to Allah, but I kept having dreams about Jesus. Every night He would visit me. He told me to follow Him."

Former Voice of the Martyrs president wrote in July 2011, "One new believer told me, 'I go to the annual pilgrimage to Mecca and walk around the Kaaba with hundreds of thousands. I will ask a man walking next to me, 'Is anyone sick in your family? Can I pray for them?' As we circle the black stone, they tell me about their illnesses or problems. I will say, 'I will pray in the name of Al Masih (Jesus, the Messiah).' I pray as we are walking. They thank me for my prayers."[2]

Since Muslim governments do not allow converts to change the religion specified on their ID cards, new believers can still go "on location" in Mecca to pray. The unchangeable government ID is considered by many as a gift from God because it means they can enter the sacred city anytime they want—or are sent.

FOUR

"Can I Worship Jesus in the Bathroom?"

Remove selected items."

Nasreen clicked the command to delete all incriminating history from her web browser. She glanced at the clock on her desktop and sighed. Her husband would be home from work in twenty minutes. He was always punctual—which helped her safely regulate time spent online. If he discovered the "shameful" sites she'd spent hours devouring, his faith in Allah would justify any retribution his outrage would care to inflict on her. She may not even be alive the next time Ahmad left home for work.

Seven children and nine years after marrying at age sixteen, Nasreen had barely been able to endure her existence. Daily overwhelmed by childcare and the unrelenting, often cruel domination of her husband, the young mother in Mecca faced the lifestyle challenges typical of any Saudi Arabian woman, but she ached for some manner of escape. Her husband's three lavish German cars offered nothing. No Muslim woman driving alone would get far enough to escape the grip of Sharia Law.

Yet Nasreen believed her longing to flee would evaporate instantly if only Ahmad would cherish her as much as he seemed to love his work. Perhaps a religion that could soothe her soul would help too. She had tried her best to remain a fervent Muslim, but the more she read her Qur'an, the more she questioned the spiritual roots of her homeland. The resulting emptiness in her heart led to desperate wanderings on the Internet.

It began as a flicker of hope two years ago when a friend told her about vacationing in London. Perhaps a family trip—to Ahmad, money would be no object—would satisfy the need to revitalize her life. Or better, her parents could keep the children while she and Ahmad romanced each other somewhere far from Mecca.

She surfed travel sites, dreaming of spots to which she could convince Ahmad to take time for a vacation. He allowed her quest but never signaled the slightest inclination to indulge her. So her vision for foreign places lost its allure. Leaving the trail of vacation travel sites in the browser history, though, offered a protective veil now that her online fantasy life had turned more dangerous. What she feared—yet hoped—most was that what she now spent hours each day reveling in would become a reality for her.

The first entry into this world apart from her colorless life happened three months into her Internet dreaming when she stumbled on a link to a website offering "Biblical Tours of the Holy Land." Within a handful of clicks, she had discovered Christianity, and her new Internet obsession began.

Nasreen read and studied the Bible on Christian sites. She

pored over online commentaries and drank in sermons posted by American preachers. Although the flood of new ideas confused her at times, she tracked down chat rooms and met people who seemed to welcome her questions rather than spurn her for them. Answer after answer satisfied her longings and encouraged even deeper questions. The Muslim mother shocked herself the first time she chatted with a man. After several interactions with Christian men, she was even more surprised to realize she never once felt afraid or intimidated by them. What she never told anyone about, though, was the dreams—until she met Rima.

"I once was a Muslim too."

Nasreen had simply stared at the words in the chat room window the first time Rima revealed why she understood Nasreen's struggle so well. From the basement of an underground ministry center in Amman, Jordan, Rima chatted with Nasreen for hours at a time. Their conversations covered everything from the Bible to marriage.

"How is it in a Christian marriage?" Nasreen wondered. "Do husbands still beat their wives once they're followers of Jesus?" Nothing was off limits in their daily sessions.

Rima told Nasreen everything about her past. Her husband had been mostly good to her. During their fifteen-year marriage, he had been a Muslim in name only, but when Rima found Jesus as her Savior, everything changed.

"Ismail was not a practicing Muslim," Rima recounted in one chat session. "He never cared about our religion. I was the one who kept Islam alive in our family. He only went to Friday prayers when his family came for a visit. The rest of the time, he couldn't have cared any less about going to the mosque.

"But when he found I was spending time with a friend who was a Jesus follower, that was it. He became a fanatic overnight. He started reading the Qur'an and made the children memorize suras. He even began morning prayers, something I never thought I would live long enough to see. His hatred for me and my faith in Jesus began to grow, and eventually he ordered me to leave. I do miss my children, but I now have Jesus."

Rima and Nasreen's chats turned into Skype calls.

"I'm telling you things I've never told anyone—not my mother or my sisters and certainly not my husband," Nasreen confessed to Rima. Finally, she summoned the courage to tell this remarkable Internet friend about her dreams. At the same time she discovered the Christian chat rooms, Nasreen had had her first dream about Jesus (who is called Isa in the Qur'an). He came to her repeatedly for a while. The encounters were so enticing that she followed each with a prayer to the only God she knew: "Oh Allah, send your prophet Isa to me to teach me again tonight." Yet as her intimacy with Rima grew, the dreams stopped. Nasreen loved her Jordanian friend but missed the mysterious prophet.

An Appointed Time

Ahmad had arrived home exactly when Nasreen expected, and the ensuing evening had passed peaceably enough. The man largely ignored his wife—and the children—as usual. After the maid left, Nasreen busied herself getting the children ready for bed. Focusing on them eased her anxiety that Ahmad might discover a website she had forgotten to delete. His time spent on the computer, though, passed without incident, and now he lay sound asleep beside her.

Nasreen was still, trying to bring her breathing back under control. That Ahmad had not stirred was a particular blessing after her outburst.

"Jesus!" she had shouted. The powerful, kind Man appeared for only an instant in her dream, but at least He had returned. His love had enveloped her once again. She turned her head to look at the bedside clock—3:13 a.m. *I will have to ask Rima about this later today,* she told herself.

Nasreen was so enchanted by the peace she felt in the aftermath of the dream that she didn't want to go back to sleep. She lay still for nearly an hour and replayed in her mind the fond memories she'd already amassed from the series of nighttime encounters with Isa.

"Nasreen, I've been praying for you to start having 'Jesus dreams' again." Rima's Skype image flickered as she continued. The two had managed to make connection early the next afternoon. "Every night I set my phone alarm so I'll wake up and pray Jesus will visit you again."

Nasreen eyed the computer screen thoughtfully. "And what time was your alarm set for last night, Rima?"

"It's strange. Normally, I set my alarm for either 3:00 or 4:00, but last night when I went to set it, for some reason the time 3:13 kept going through my head." Rima paused, leaned toward her computer screen, and wondered at the tears brimming in Nasreen's eyes. "Are you all right?"

Nasreen gulped a breath. "That's when I saw Jesus last night."

Rima glanced at her keyboard, then looked straight at the

camera and pointed to Nasreen. "'Blessed are those who find wisdom, those who gain understanding.'"

"What?"

"'Blessed are those who find wisdom, those who gain understanding.' It's a proverb I memorized last week."

"From the Bible?"

"Yes, Nasreen. It's for you."

"How do you know?"

"The verse number. It's Proverbs *3:13*. Jesus has come to bless you with wisdom from Him and understanding of His purpose for your life."

Nasreen closed her eyes. She lowered her head and covered her mouth with her right hand. Her shoulders trembled almost imperceptibly. Rima watched tears drip from Nasreen's face as the two women sat in silence for several minutes. The significance of the return of Nasreen's Jesus dreams and of the proverb was instantly obvious to Rima. Her friend's visitations had not always been a blessing, and perhaps this renewal meant the good was winning out. Jesus wasn't the only one who had visited Nasreen at night.

VISITS FROM THE *Jinn*—AND JESUS

In Arabia, jinn are also called the "little people." They're romanticized and dubbed "genies" in movies like Aladdin and Ali Baba and the Forty Thieves, but the Hollywood depiction of these beings from another dimension is an insipid distraction from the real, satanic versions that had plagued Nasreen and countless Arabs before her.

"Since I was a young girl," Nasreen had told Rima, "I shuddered whenever they came. My dreams of them were twisted and cruel. The jinn often scorned me, laughing and laughing as if I was the most meaningless creature in the universe. I've seen them at the Kaaba too. It seems they're everywhere. And now they're after me, more than ever. They even torment my family. My two daughters have run screaming into my bedroom, unable to talk. Rima, could this be connected to our talks about Jesus?"

Rima feared that was exactly the problem, and she worried that the jinn might frighten Nasreen away from the real Lord. Just after her Jesus dreams stopped, Nasreen told Rima of the most terrifying jinn encounter yet.

"The other night was the worst, Rima. I thought I would die. The hideous thing woke me up. It wasn't a dream. He was in my room! I smelled fire, and there he was . . . sitting on my chest! I couldn't breathe, and I couldn't say a word. I can't get out of my mind his revolting red hair and the ruthless evil in his eyes."

"There's a war for your soul, Nasreen," Rima had told her. "The jinn are just foot soldiers for the one who sent them. Satan wants to intimidate you. Don't let him do that."

Rima recalled the young woman's determined response. "I know about courage. I've had to act as if my marriage was fulfilling and my life was perfect for years. Living in Mecca means we put on a good show. Rima, you and I have been visiting for almost a year now. I've asked you everything I can think of. You're closer to me than my five sisters. You know all my secrets."

A flicker of the Skype image jarred Rima away from her recollections. As Nasreen wiped the tears from her eyes, Rima saw the same fearlessness as during that last talk about the jinn. At least there had been no jinn after that. Yet now Rima could tell something more was coming.

"Rima, do you remember when I said I'd told you all of my secrets?"

"Yes, Nasreen. I do. I was honored to hear you say that."

"Well, now I have another. One that wasn't mine to tell before."

Rima looked quietly at her friend's image on the computer screen.

"Rima, I am following Jesus now. I loved Him right away, but I wasn't sure what I was supposed to do about that. After He came to me in dreams, you explained each message He gave me. I just couldn't resist Him after He showed me so much love. I do have another question, though."

Rima drooped forward, relieved that her friend had not abandoned the quest to know the truth about God. "What is it, Nasreen?"

"You're not the only one who's been telling me about Jesus. For weeks now, I've been listening to Trans World Radio almost every night. It reaches all the way to Mecca with wonderful teachings about Jesus. I just can't get enough of Him on the Internet during the day, so after dinner I go into the bathroom. I keep a small radio hidden there behind a pillow so I can listen to people talking about my Jesus. I am learning so much, but . . ."

"But what, Nasreen?"

"Rima." Her friend paused and looked sheepishly at the computer. "Is it okay to worship Jesus in the bathroom?"

Rima smiled. "Yes, Nasreen. It's very okay. He understands."

AFTERWORD

Nasreen had wanted out of Islam—and out of her marriage. In the world's most hostile city toward Christianity, either dream could get her executed. Now that she knows Jesus, though, she wants to stay in her marriage. She's praying that her husband will have Jesus dreams too. If they come in time, she may live to see her husband and her marriage transformed by Christ.

FIVE

A Martyr's Final Poem

J ust how dangerous is it to follow Jesus in Saudi Arabia? Fatima al-Mutairi found out. She lived in Buraydah, a city known for Islamic fanaticism that outstrips even most places in the rest of Saudi Arabia. At age twenty-six, Fatima left this world, a martyr for Christ. Her own brother killed her, but the nightmarish story ends with an inspiring vision of hope.

FOR A NAME'S SAKE

The prophet Muhammad named his fourth daughter Fatima. During the prophet's wars and several attempts on his life, this courageous woman remained steadfastly faithful to her father. She so esteemed Muhammad, in fact, that his death literally took the life out of Fatima, and she passed away a few months after the prophet died. As a result, she is still honored as an example of strength and courage for all Muslims, and her revered name is used generously by Muslim parents, who often compare her to Mary the mother of Jesus. To be named Fatima is an honor for any Muslim girl—especially if that girl lives in Saudi Arabia and inherits an honorable bloodline.

Fatima al-Mutairi belonged to a renowned Bedouin tribe with centuries-old roots in Saudi Arabia. The al-Mutairis' influence spans the whole Kingdom of Saud and spills into neighboring Kuwait as well. It was natural that an al-Mutairi daughter from the eastern province of Saudi Arabia would be given the name Fatima. All strident Muslims, her family includes a brother who is both a Muslim cleric and a member of Saudi Arabia's Commission of the Promotion of Virtue and the Prevention of Vice (not much explanation needed to know what that's all about). Given the girl's heritage, then, and her pristine Islamic upbringing, the al-Mutairi clan expected many things from Fatima. But becoming a Jesus follower was not one of them.

DREAMS—AGAIN

How many people had Fatima met on the Internet who claimed to have dreams about Jesus? And most of them Muslim! At first, she tried to explain them away, but the dream stories awakened her curiosity about the spiritual world outside of Islam. She began to read everything she could find about Jesus, and her Internet friends—she truly felt that's what they were—enjoyed discussing the countless questions she raised about their faith. And it seemed that every day she met yet another person who had dreamed about this Jesus. Each one recounted a powerful, gentle Person who overwhelmed him or her, not with unendurable shame as the Muslim leaders did, but with a pure love that reached deep inside. This idea of a loving God is what astounded her. One friend described Him as a shepherd watching over and caring for His sheep. Fatima's soul ached for such an experience of belonging and acceptance.

For months, the young woman pored over the New Testament online and saw for herself the glorious love of Jesus for His disciples. He was irresistible, and one night she bowed in obedience to His call on her life. She agreed to follow Him, whatever the consequences might—or most certainly would—be. Although Fatima never went to a church, she prayed almost every day online with believers around the world who encouraged her with their own stories of struggling against family and friends in their journey with Christ.

Fatima was true to her name even as an "infidel." Her faith in Christ deepened rapidly, and her passion for the Lord became well-known among online believers. She joined the Gulf Christian Forum, a group of just ten resolute Christians who flood the Internet with e-mails and blogs declaring Christ to any Muslims who will pay attention. Every night Fatima fielded questions from Muslims searching for the truth about God, and blog by blog, her penname "Rania" became famous for her inspiring poetry about Jesus.

INCRIMINATING WORDS

Fatima was at work the day her brother found her journals. Although the apostasy was obvious, he rummaged through every possible hiding place in her room to find even more evidence. He discovered the Christian contacts on her computer, Bible study notes she'd written for herself, and finally, the poems about Jesus. This disgrace was unthinkable. Only one solution could spare his family from shame that could pollute generations of al-Mutairis to come.

When Fatima returned home, her brother announced to the family that she had devoted herself to the infidel faith, a faith for which she would now die. To confirm the stunning revelation, the raging cleric asked Fatima, "Are you a Jesus follower?"

Her answer was simple: "Yes. Yes I am."

He took her cell phone, so she could not call for help—not that anyone in Buraydah would have come to her rescue—and locked Fatima in her bedroom. For the four hours she awaited her execution, the computer that had brought Christ to her brought Rania's last words to the world. To her online church and beyond, she sent out one last poem on the Internet:

> May the Lord Jesus guide you, O Muslims, and enlighten your hearts that you might love others. We do not worship the cross, and we are not insane. We worship the Lord Jesus, the light of the world.
>
> We left Muhammad, and we are no longer on his path. We follow Jesus the Messiah, the clear truth. And truly we love our homeland, and we are not traitors. We take pride that we are Saudi citizens. How could we betray our homeland and our dear people?? How could we, when for death for Saudi, we are ready???
>
> The homeland of my grandfathers and their glories are for which I am writing these odes. And we say, "Proud, proud,

proud we are to be Saudis." We chose our way, the way of the guided. And every man is free to choose which religion.

Be content to leave us alone to be believers in Jesus. Leave us to live in grace until our time comes. My tears are on my cheek and, oh! The heart is sad for those who became Christians, how you are so cruel!

And the Messiah says: "Blessed are the persecuted." And we for the sake of Christ all things bear. What is it to you that we are infidels?

Enough—your swords do not concern me, nor evil, nor disgrace. Your threats do not trouble me, and we are not afraid.

And by God, I am unto death a Christian—verily I cry for what passed by of a sad life. I was far from the Lord Jesus for many years.

Oh History, record and bear witness, Oh witnesses! We are, Christians—in the path of Christ we tread.

Take from me this word, and note it well. You see Jesus is my Lord, and He is the Best of Protectors.

I advise you to pity yourself, to clap your hands in mourning. See your ugly hatred look.

Where is the humanity, the love, where are you?

As to my last words, I pray to the Lord of the worlds.

Jesus is the Messiah, the Light of clear Guidance. That He changes notions, and sets the scales of justice aright.

And that He spread Love among you, Oh Muslims.

Minutes after she clicked Send for the last time, Fatima's brother entered the room. He beat her cruelly, breaking bones and rupturing skin. Finally, he cut out her tongue and dragged her outside where he burned her alive.

Thoughts on a Martyr's Death

I suspect Fatima received a hero's welcome in heaven. Her love for Jesus matched the passion with which she had searched for Him. Steeped more deeply in Islam than most people could ever be, her life and death shout the reality of a Savior whose loving power overwhelms even the gravest deceptions of Satan. Fatima, the brave young saint, was true to her name meaning "courage and strength" even in death.

One day in heaven, I hope Jesus will give us all the honor of meeting Fatima—martyr for Christ in Saudi Arabia.

SIX

Bible Study in Mecca

The hajj is one of Five Pillars of Faith for Islam. Each pillar is a "faith essential," which means that making pilgrimage to Mecca is the accepted confirmation of a person's Muslim faith.

Every Muslim is expected to "make the hajj" once in his or her lifetime or at least to send a family member as proxy. About two million make the pilgrimage to Islam's holiest city each year. This is not only their greatest dream but also their ultimate destination in life. Muslims literally live to make the hajj. While there, thousands sleep in makeshift tents all over the city. It looks like an Arabic version of the Feast of Tabernacles.

One Visitor to Mecca—whether during the hajj or not—consistently gets into the city without identification papers. Jesus has been dropping in for centuries, and lately He seems to be taking up residence there. His message of grace arrives quietly in Mecca. It has to. But like a palm tree that flourishes in the desert and yields sweet dates despite harsh conditions, His Word has taken root and is growing. Although "officially" there are only Muslims in Mecca, followers of Jesus study Scripture there every day—many of them thanks to a woman who risks everything for the sake of His Word.

REAL FAITH AMID THE FAITHFUL

Aisha lay still, listening. The fabric of the tent around her delineated the quiet world of her family inside from the drone of a hundred thousand pilgrims overflowing the streets outside. The patchwork habitat offered barely enough space to walk between shelters, so nearby sounds—mostly snores and the heavy breathing of sleep—separated from the background murmur. Two tents over, she heard the subdued repetitions of a late-night prayer.

Aisha rolled her head to the side and looked at her sister as the younger girl sighed lazily. Typically, her sister would have been the one wanting to stay up late, if only because their parents insisted the younger family members go to bed early. But tonight Aisha's eyes remained open. Why, she wondered, did she simply not want to sleep? Today she had endured seven exhausting circuits of the Kaaba stone. Her feet still tingled, reminding her of the abuse her heels and toes had suffered in the trampling crowds. And in the morning, the family would rise at dawn in hopes of catching an early shuttle to Mina for the next adventure of her second hajj. Yes, sleep tonight was badly needed.

From somewhere nearby, a young voice shouted, "I don't want to, Mama!" Aisha chuckled at what a child's dream can reveal, but another sound, much closer, cut short her amusement. She sat up, expecting to see a knife slitting the tent canvas near her feet. What she saw was even more shocking.

A Man in a gleaming white robe—something other than a dishdasha—stood over her. She glanced behind Him at the tent and saw that He had not cut an opening to get in. He raised a hand, as if in greeting but also to calm her. No one else stirred.

Light from the Man's clothing seemed to flow into her body. Her first thought had been that some cleric had sought out her family—or more frightening, perhaps just her. Yet an unearthly warmth emanated from this Man. She instantly knew He loved her deeply. And in that instant, she also knew who He was. Jesus stood in her tent.

He stepped backward and ducked as if stooping to exit the tent's low doorway. As He faded through the side, the girl glimpsed His eyes. *Come with Me*, they seemed to say.

Aisha sat staring, openmouthed, at the tent wall. Perhaps sounds continued in the night around her, but Aisha did not hear them. For an hour, she neither moved nor spoke a word. What could be more dangerous than having a vision of Jesus in Mecca during the hajj?

A month later, Aisha and her family took their next trip, this time out of the country. Far less momentous but vastly more enjoyable than a pilgrimage to Mecca: they visited Aisha's favorite relatives in Jordan.

One night at her cousin's home while channel surfing before going to bed, Aisha froze at the words from a Christian station in Egypt.

"Some of you have had a vision of Jesus," the Egyptian preacher called—to her? "Be thankful He has selected you for this high honor! Jesus doesn't waste time with these visits. He is calling you to follow Him. He has a purpose for your life."

Aisha again found herself speechless because of Jesus. And again, she told no one. After she returned to Saudi Arabia, though, she discovered just how determined this Man from heaven seemed to be with His purposes for her.

The new visions were different than the one in Mecca. He didn't call on her only at night. Jesus even met her in broad daylight. Sometimes she saw only His face, and He never spoke. But every time, the message she saw in His eyes was the same: *Come with Me.*

HEMMED IN

Three months had passed since her family's last visit to the relatives in Jordan, and this time, Aisha felt a boldness growing in her heart to reveal her intriguing, otherworldly journey. She also sensed something different about her cousin Reem. In fact, Reem had been the first to mention "spiritual encounters." So alone one evening in Reem's bedroom, Aisha took advantage of the opening.

"Are you having dreams about Muhammad?" Aisha tested the waters with her question.

Reem's eyes roamed the floor of her bedroom, choosing the words for her answer. "No, Aisha. Actually, it hasn't been Muhammad." Head still angled to the floor, she raised only her eyes and peered steadily from under her brow at Aisha. "They are about Jesus." She gauged her cousin's reaction and then went on. "I have had several now. I can't describe the incredible peace I've had when He was speaking to me." Reem held her breath, hoping she had correctly assessed her cousin and friend's willingness to hear the truth without reproach.

Aisha eyed Reem calmly. "I know exactly what you mean." The corners of her mouth hinted at a smile. "I have them too."

Reem raised her head and faced Aisha. "Wow," was all she said.

Aisha showered her cousin with details about her astounding Jesus encounters. Reem had met with Jesus, too, and each time felt drawn to some purpose—a mission—for their newfound Savior.

To explore questions that had dominated their private thoughts, they spent the remaining days of Aisha's visit in as much seclusion as they could come by without mustering unwanted, potentially dangerous questions from others in the family:

Why was Jesus appearing to them?

What was it in each encounter that brought them such peace and security?

Why was Jesus giving the two of them such similar visitations?

One question, though, seemed more urgent than any of the others: *How was the Injil—the New Testament—hidden in Reem's dresser different from any other book?* The question about its divine origin helped the two young women put into words what both already knew in their hearts. It also led them to the exact nature of the mission to which they both felt called.

While Christian literature of any kind is forbidden in Saudi Arabia, Bibles remain readily available in Jordan. Reem's New Testament had not been hard to come by. They would find a way to smuggle them into Saudi Arabia!

The close ties between Reem's family and Aisha's became the platform for their ministry. During visits the following year, the cousins crafted a plan, and despite the extreme risks—especially to Aisha—put it into action.

Reem's diminutive edition of the New Testament not only fit inconspicuously in Reem's sock drawer, but they found, thanks to

Reem's skills as a seamstress, that it could be sewn into the hem of a hijab. Their mission was in business.

RISK/REWARD—IN HER OWN WORDS

When Aisha told me her story on one of my visits to Jordan, she left me with this statement of vision and courage about what her mission to Mecca is accomplishing:

> The Bibles sewn into my hijab are uncomfortable. But I get twenty Injils each trip to Jordan. Reem is our seamstress, and I bring them straight to my home in Mecca. So far government authorities have not questioned me even once. I know they would kill me if they discovered what I'm doing. And even though I never tell anyone about the books, they are gone the day I arrive home. The Word of God is the most priceless possession in Mecca.

PART · III

IRAN—WHY AHMADINEJAD CAN'T SLEEP AT NIGHT

SEVEN

One Tough Burka

Mahmoud Ahmadinejad won a stunning victory in Iran's 2009 presidential election—stunning not only because of the landslide proportions of his win but also because of the flagrant crookedness of the means by which he achieved victory. Thousands of Iranians smelled a rotten kabob (in Esfahan, for example, more votes were recorded in favor of Ahmadinejad than the entire population of the city), and they took to the streets across Iran to protest the bogus election. Mostly the under-thirty crowd, protesters were fed up with the corruption in Iran's government.

When the country's Guardian Council certified and sealed the election on June 12, 2009, Iran exploded. "The Persian Awakening," also called "The Green Revolution" by some, was more than simply a revolt against the election. It was fury at three decades of repression and cruelty under the Islamic Republic of Iran. The country's younger crowd had never known anything but the brutality and corruption of the regimes led by Ayatollah Ali Khamenei and his predecessor.

True to form, the government fought the dissension ruthlessly. Just as the 1989 faceoff between a lone man and a line of tanks in Tiananmen Square became the symbol of freedom for that generation of Chinese, a sixteen-year-old woman offered the rally point for Iranians in 2009. Neda Soltan, however, did not fare as well as the brave young Chinese protester. As Neda joined companions in protest on the streets of Tehran, a government sniper shot the fun-loving, aspiring singer through the heart. While the young woman bled to death in her father's arms, a nearby witness recorded the cruel event on a cell phone and e-mailed the video to a friend in Holland who posted the scene on Facebook for the world to see within five minutes of Neda's last breath. The Islamic Republic of Iran was caught red-handed.

Supporters dubbed Neda "The Angel of Iran," and some news sources claim that more people watched Neda's death than many of the biggest news stories in the last ten years. Within hours, pictures of Neda appeared on posters at marches in Los Angeles and New York. Firsthand observers claim that, although not visible on the video, Neda was wearing a hidden cross forced out from under her shirt by the bullet that killed her. The very public story of Neda Soltan, however, is no more remarkable than many more private miracles happening among the women and men of Iran.

BIG BROTHER'S BIG SISTER

"You Christians are going to hell!"

Dina screamed at Hormoz Shariat and would have done everything in her substantial power to hasten his departure from this life if she could have. Shariat, though, sat safely in front of a television camera on the opposite side of the globe.

The winsome host of the call-in satellite TV program for evangelizing Muslims, *Iran Alive!*, was accustomed to Dina's ranting. She was a regular caller. But had Hormoz been sitting closer to Dina—anywhere within the borders of Iran, in fact—he may not have handled her attack so serenely.

And had Dina been in Los Angeles with Hormoz and willing to practice local customs, she would have presented significant competition for any California girl in typical beachwear. She looked like a model from head to toe. She was thoroughly Muslim. She was a ranking official in Iran's Female Secret Police (FSP).

A specialized division of the national Morality Police, the FSP torments violators of Sharia Law. Working undercover, Dina and her teams hunted women who let so much as a strand of hair slip out from under the required hijab. Dina's only conscience was for strict adherence to Sharia. She'd watched women endure as many as eighty lashes for violating codes of modesty, and the beatings suffered by those she arrested never bothered her—until she called Hormoz once too often.

"I pity you Christians because your destiny is hell," Dina continued, confident but without pity. "Islam is the only way, and Christians are in a false religion. In the end you will pay for this. Allah will send you into the flames."

"Dina, whenever you call me, you sound angry and filled with hatred. I think your religion produces that in you."

"I can never have a better life than I have had in Islam," Dina spat across the world.

"Oh? Has Islam brought you any particular happiness that

you can point to?" Hormoz folded his hands under his chin and tipped forward in his chair. He glanced at the studio floor, then smiled softly into the camera, waiting for Dina's response.

"There are other problems not connected to my religion that I am experiencing now." Her voice dropped.

"Would you like to tell me more about those problems, Dina?"

"Why would I tell you? You can do nothing for me!"

"Have you ever considered the possibility that you can have a better life?" Hormoz paused. "Jesus can give it to you. He did that for me and for thousands of people in Iran just like you, Dina."

For Hormoz, 1979 had been a year to rejoice. The revolution in Iran sealed the country's destiny as the world's foremost guardian of Islam. *Death to America, death to Christians* had been his favorite words. But the crushing reality of Sharia Law in action quickly snuffed out all enthusiasm for his country's new way of life.

He found an exit in the form of a visiting woman from California. Soon after he married Donnell, the two moved to Los Angeles. Hormoz began graduate school at USC, where he fell in love for the second time—with the United States of America.

Although several believers reached out to them soon after the Shariats arrived, Hormoz was not an easy target. He had taken part in the great Islamic revolution and still harbored the belief that Muhammad's ways were the path to Allah. Somewhere—and perhaps he would yet live to see the day—the truth would work out in accord with the prophet's real intentions.

Before that day, though, the ways of a different prophet took hold in Hormoz's heart. The Shariats welcomed Christ into their lives and bore an immediate burden for countless Iranians with little or no access to the truth of Christianity. Their compassion birthed a television program to reach Muslims in Iran. They knew that, of the country's seventy-five million inhabitants, forty-five million have access to satellite channels, despite periodic raids by government authorities to purge them. From the moment Hormoz first beamed his intrusion into the Muslim realm from a secret location in America his program was a success. The charismatic smile and challenging rhetoric of this man from nowhere fascinated a restless, yearning, mostly under-thirty audience of beleaguered Iranians.

FACEOFF

"I am not married, and my mother is suffering with cancer." Dina's words sounded to Hormoz like a confession. "She's bedridden and is going to die soon. The doctors cannot do anything else for her." Dina paused. Hormoz could not quite tell if she was holding back tears. "I have no one else."

"I'm sorry to hear that, Dina. What will you do now?"

"We have both decided to kill ourselves tonight."

Hormoz had heard admissions of cruelty, doubt, adultery, and assorted perversions, but he was not prepared for this. The smile dropped from his face.

"This will be a first for you, Hormoz, won't it?" Dina's vengeful spirit returned. "We are going to commit suicide right now, on your program. I only wish *you* could watch *me*. At least my mother and I will go to heaven—which is more than I could say for a pathetic Christian like you and others who watch your program! What do you have to say to that?"

Hormoz leaned back in his chair and stared for several seconds into the camera without speaking.

"That is really sad to hear, Dina." Hormoz's face was serious, but his eyes smiled at the young woman trapped in a wretched world nearly eight thousand miles away. "But since you're going to kill yourself anyway, why don't you give Jesus a week? If He doesn't answer a single prayer for you or do anything in your life in seven days, then just go ahead and kill yourself. That's what you were going to do anyway. You have nothing to lose."

Hormoz paused to heighten the effect of the gauntlet he'd thrown before the Morality Policewoman. "But I'm sure you're afraid to try this—aren't you, Dina?"

"I'm not afraid of anything you dare me to do! The Christian God is a false God. He is incapable of giving me anything I pray for, because He is not there! Only Allah can answer prayers."

"And how is he doing with answering your prayers right now?"

"Are you trying to be funny? You're mocking my pain."

"I am not mocking you, Dina. I'm as serious as I can be."

The voice on the phone rose in self-defense. "Jesus was only a prophet. He can't do anything. You're fooling yourself—and trying to fool me!"

Hormoz chuckled. "I knew you were afraid."

"Okay, then. I know you're just playing with me, but I accept your foolish challenge. What do I do for a week? Whatever it is will be a waste of time." Dina knew she had the better of Hormoz now. "I'll wait a week, and then come back and kill myself on your program—*if* you are brave enough to take my next call."

"Dina, I promise to take your call, but you must do something for me first."

"What is that?"

"Pray, and ask Jesus to be your Savior." Hormoz's eyes still smiled, but his face showed he was not at all toying with his desperate caller.

"What! How can I do that?"

"It's simple, Dina. I'm going to lead you in a prayer, word by word, and you just repeat after me."

"I don't believe this. How can you ask me to do such a thing?"

"It's part of our bargain, Dina." Without waiting for further response, Hormoz pushed on, "'Dear Jesus' . . . Say it, Dina."

The voice on the line laughed. "I can't believe that I'm actually doing this!"

"Dina! 'Dear Jesus . . .'"

"Dear Jesus . . ."

The Dungeon of Tehran

Dina hated only one thing more than a Muslim who compromised standards of decency and morality: a Muslim who dared convert to Christianity. This passion solidified her position with superiors in the Morality Police. Secretly alarmed at the defections to the Christian God, Islamic leaders demanded control over deviant Iranians. Public declarations aside, conversions to Christ mushroomed in Iran as in other Muslim nations, making Christianity truly the fastest-growing religion in the world. Yet Dina and her comrades believed they had a solution. As converts and other political offenders found themselves in Evin Prison, one by one they would stem the tide of apostasy.

While not personally involved in the raid, Dina relished the news that on the day before the Christians' favorite celebration, Christmas Eve, in 2010, seventy Iranian house-church leaders were rounded up, arrested, and put away in Evin Prison. A person would renounce any faith to be set free from such an earthly hell.

Looming over the north side of Tehran in the Alborz Mountains, Evin Prison brings human pain and misery to an unmatched level of perfection. Dina's visits there reassured her that perpetrators were treated in the manner deserving of their crimes. But even she had required several duty calls to thoroughly harden her heart to the horrors of the place.

Although she had pushed her way indifferently through crowds wailing outside for incarcerated loved ones, Dina retched involuntarily at the stench the first time she stepped within Evin's walls. She immediately recognized the need to keep the prison's deeper secrets. Average citizens could never understand the necessity of a place like this. And because of this special knowledge, she was incensed when a visitor dared to make public the photos he had snapped, unseen, with his cell phone.

The images showed five men dangling from wires thirty feet above the floor of the main cell block. Their inevitably soiled pants and disjointed hands and feet evidenced the two days of abuse that would end in their slow, ghastly deaths.

There were other stories Dina also knew to be true. Guards found unique, eternal punishments for women in the prison. Young, attractive ones fared the worst. Prison officials routinely raped girls before executing them. The torment in the here and now was surpassed only by the feared result this would conjure in the minds of the assaulted women. Only virgins were assured of quick entry into heaven, and guards laughed while raping and defiling young girls before they were executed. Had they done nothing else in life to deserve hell, that one act would keep them out of paradise!

For a time, Dina's self-conditioning kept at bay any questions she might otherwise consider regarding the rightness of the Evin solution. It was *sigheh*, though, that finally managed to sow doubts in her worldview.

To avoid the brutal fate of most female inmates, the more beautiful women make deals with their captors to secure freedom. They offer themselves in *sigheh*, a "temporary marriage" sanctioned by Sharia Law and blessed by Iranian mullahs, the spiritual authorities on all things Muslim. *Sigheh* allows a man to "marry" a woman—whether or not he already has a wife—solely for the purpose of having sex with the new woman for a short time. Even outside the prison, this authorized prostitution is often the only way a divorced woman can survive.

What pierced Dina's conscience was the blatant opportunism of *sigheh* at the Alborz Mountain dungeon. Prison workers inside and mullahs themselves on the outside trafficked endlessly in helpless women to feed the hypocritical lusts of powerful men. Dina could not deny that part of her job was to feed an evil system the mullahs had set up for their own pleasures. She believed their actions had nothing to do with the correct following of Islam. Yet these were her religious leaders. The irreconcilable conflict grew within her, and thoughts of suicide began to appeal.

DEATH DEFIED

"Who is it?" Dina screamed at the footsteps she feared belonged to an intruder in the house.

It was early morning of the fifth day since Hormoz promised Jesus would help her, and she was still waiting. How ironic would it be if the only response to her prayer was a burglar—or a government colleague coming to take her to Evin Prison for participating in an illegal television show? That would keep her from fulfilling *her* promise to entertain Hormoz's audience with her death. She squinted at the thought.

Dina's mother peeked through the door to her daughter's room. A peaceful smile spread across the older woman's lips. "It's just me, Dina."

A thief would have shocked Dina less. The daughter's eyes snapped open. "Mother! What are you doing? How did you get out of bed?"

"Dina, last night after you turned off my light, I thought, *I will die tonight.* It frightened me, so I wondered which imam I should pray to one last time. Then I saw His face. Right there in my room." Her gaze drifted from Dina's face to the floor.

"Which one was it, Mother?"

The woman closed her eyes and then looked at her daughter. "Dina, it wasn't an imam. It was . . . Jesus."

Dina stared at her mother for several seconds. She was appalled yet grateful at the same instant, and the conflict within her subsided quickly as something remarkable occurred to Dina: it was the answer she had expected.

"I woke up a few minutes ago and realized I felt no pain. Not even a little. All of it was gone."

Her mother's agony had been unbearable for months. If nothing else had happened, Dina knew the relief alone was a miracle.

"Not only that. I could move comfortably and felt so peaceful that I decided to try to stand up. Dina, I could walk! I can hardly say it, but . . . I feel well again."

Dina rose slowly from her bed. Before she could step close enough to hug her mother, the policewoman melted in tears. Dina had not told her about the prayer with Hormoz. They had much to talk about over breakfast.

Hormoz finished another call. His eyes widened as the name of the next caller came up on the screen. He glanced at Donnell, who monitored the incoming calls just off camera. Eyes matching his, she nodded and mouthed, "Yes, it's Dina."

"Welcome back, Dina. How are you?"

"Hormoz, last week I repeated the words you told me to say, but I didn't take them seriously." The TV host nodded into the camera as Dina continued. "But God did. Tonight my mother is with me again. She's *standing* here beside me!"

This time, it was Hormoz who struggled to hold back tears. "And?"

"I didn't want Jesus to be the answer. All week long, I thought of everything in my life that was negative. I was trying to feel depressed. But each time I tried to concentrate on my problems, I was flooded with peace. I would stop by the mirror, amazed at the smile on my face. As for my mother, she's well, Hormoz. She's well! And so am I! Jesus is everything you promised. Thank you, my friend."

AFTERWORD

Hormoz recounts, "Dina's salvation experience generated unprecedented interest in the power of prayer. Even though she didn't believe a word of what she prayed that night on television, God intervened anyway. Now Muslims call in regularly to ask us to pray for them. Dina's story connected with people because they grasped Jesus' forgiveness. They had heard all the names Dina called Jesus and His followers, yet Jesus welcomed the woman into His family."

The remarkable success of Hormoz's broadcast continues. An estimated seven to nine million Iranians—10 percent of the population—watch his television program regularly. He has garnered the nickname "The Billy Graham of Iran."

Although satellite dishes are illegal in Iran, most people have one anyway. It seems that the more the government wants to block a program, the more Iranians want to watch it. They prefer most anything to the standard government programing. After all, how many times can you stomach a rerun of Ahmadinejad's latest speech? Dina's mother remains healed of cancer, and Dina is now married to another former Muslim. She resigned discreetly from the Morality Police and now hunts Muslim women with whom she can share the gospel. Her location cannot be disclosed due to the number of threats on her life, but I saw her once when Hormoz and I were traveling together in the Middle East.

The restaurant was packed with Iranian believers eating, laughing, and telling stories. Hormoz waved at a woman in her early thirties, and the energetic lady smiled and made her way toward us. Dressed sharply in jeans and a colorful blouse, she was as striking as her outfit. On the way to our table, she stopped at least five times to give hugs and share kind words with people along the way.

"Hi, I'm Dina!" I had heard her story but didn't realized she was the one Hormoz had summoned to our table. My jaw dropped.

"It's a pleasure to meet you." Dina reached for my hand. "We're glad to have you with us. Iranian believers love Americans. You're welcome here. And by the way," Dina pointed across the room. "That's my mom over there, waving at you."

EIGHT

Nukes, Imams, and the Underground Sheikh

W hile writing a high school research paper, my daughter, Sarah, once asked me to tell her the difference between Sunni and Shiite Muslims. When I explained that they are the two major divisions within the religion of Islam, she observed that it must be similar to having various denominations within Christianity. She was on the right track, but to sharpen her perspective a bit, I offered one key distinction: when the Methodists disagree with the Baptists, they don't set off car bombs in the Baptist church parking lot!

Sunnis and Shiites likely think trying to destroy one another is acceptable because neither believes the other group is truly Muslim. I witnessed an amusing demonstration of this one afternoon while visiting Lebanon. Two clerics, charged with the responsibility to call Muslims to their daily prayers, blared at one another from the loudspeakers of their respective minarets:

"Sunni Islam is the only true Islam!"

"Sunni Islam is the slave of Shia Islam!"

"Shiites are apostates!"

"Sunnis are going to hell!"

The split between the two began centuries ago over determining the successor to Muhammad. Sunnis believe the next in line was Abu Bakr, but he was not one of Muhammad's offspring. To Shiites, the blood relationship was paramount, and Ali ibn Abi Talib was their man. Through the years, Sunnis seem to have gotten their way with most Muslims. But while they claim the lion's share of adherents—80 to 90 percent of Muslims worldwide—the Shia are clearly the lion's roar. And for assuring both vigilance and virulence of Shiite followers, the Iranians have just the place to do it.

There's No Place like Qom

If Iran's deadliest, most technologically sophisticated military installation and its largest, most influential theological center were on opposite sides of the country, either could be a grave threat to peace in the Middle East. But place them side by side, and you have a combination ready to topple the stability of the entire world at a moment's notice.

A dozen or so miles north of Qom, the world's largest training center for Shia Islam, lies Fordo, Iran's nuclear (weapons) development facility.[1] The proximity of the two represents the close tie between Shiite Muslim theology and its intent to dominate the world.

Since the Iranian Revolution in 1979, the population of Qom has tripled. The massive influx has been fueled by the presence of more than fifty Islamic seminaries. The city of roughly one million people employs forty-five thousand Muslim clerics, and many of Iran's "grand ayatollahs" maintain offices in both Tehran, the nation's capital, and Qom.

Although its spectacular growth has happened within thirty years, the city has been a hub for Shiites since the early 1500s. At any given time in Qom some fifty thousand seminarians study in its schools, heightening its worldwide influence. Pakistan alone has six thousand students in Qom. There are even study programs for women who want to deepen their understanding of the Muslim faith. Virtually every high-ranking religious leader in Shia Islam has studied in Qom, and much of the money that comes from "alms" ends up here. According to one of the Five Pillars of the Islamic Faith, Muslims are required give alms annually. This mandate, along with the significant proportion of Iran's tax revenue funneled to Qom, results in an ongoing flood of wealth into the city.

Outlying Fordo receives its share and puts it to use at the town's notorious uranium enrichment facility. But the danger to the world is due as much to the nuclear fuel refined beneath the suburban hills of Fordo as to the fanatical energy that flows there from Qom. Neither is a friendly place to be a Christian—especially for a Muslim cleric who meets Jesus there. It's enough to drive a believer . . . underground.

MUSLIM ON THE SURFACE

Only one place would suit a brilliant, well-connected student like Ali. His mentors all agreed that this stellar young Shiite must study at Qom—and he did not disappoint them.

No course was too arduous nor regimen too grueling for the

celebrated scholar-in-the-making. By the time he graduated, he had memorized most of the Qur'an and so impressed his teachers that they launched him ahead of his classmates, grooming him to be a regional leader whose influence would push forward the cause of Shia domination far beyond the borders of Iran. What an asset he would be in the Shiite master plan to infiltrate Sunni Arab nations and gain control.

The accolades and trust placed in him by his elders suited the young sheikh's bloodline, his educational performance, his theological expertise, and his drive to excel. The one thing it did not suit was Ali's true faith. Beneath the surface of Ali's public life, an unseen force had intervened. None of his professors, no matter how astute, would ever have guessed that the one-in-a-thousand seminarian had had a personal introduction to Jesus Christ.

Ali met Jesus in Qom. After a half-dozen visitations, the young man could hardly endure the unanswered questions swirling in his mind. Why was this prophet appearing to him? What was the meaning of His messages about salvation? Was Jesus something more than Ali's lifelong faith in the teachings of Muhammad had led him to believe?

Seminary studies took him deeper into the Qur'an than he had ever gone before, yet nothing spoke to any of his wonderings. He lay awake one night, propped on his elbows in bed, mulling over the problem of his unanswered questions, when an obvious possibility surfaced in his mind. How had he missed it before? *The Qur'an speaks of Jesus, true enough, but there is another book.* The Christian Bible would certainly have much to say about Him—if it could be trusted.

Ali's drive to understand his visions overwhelmed any doubts he had about checking out the Christian writings. Satisfied that he knew what the next step in his search would be, Ali let the pillow engulf his head. For the first time in several weeks, he rested well that night. But as he drifted into sleep, Ali startled at the thought of one final question: how would he get a Bible in Qom?

PILGRIM TO TEHRAN

Sipping coffee the next morning alone in his kitchen, Ali arrived at the first part of an answer to the previous night's question: he wouldn't. There would be no Bible for him in Qom. Even if one existed somewhere, he wouldn't dare seek it out. And wherever else he might go to find a Bible, he must be discreet. Leaving Qom for any undisclosed purpose would raise questions from fellow students and instructors. He had no desire to tarnish his image as a model Muslim.

With the first taste of his second cup came the idea that set him on a pilgrimage to find out just what Jesus wanted of him: *my parents.* What could be more perfect? A trip to see one's father and mother is natural any time for any student—and his parents' next-door neighbor was an Armenian and a Christian. If Ali were to drop in to see Jivan while in Tehran? He would be sure to have a Bible Ali could borrow.

Two weeks later, Ali stood in Jivan's living room. Although the neighbor seemed surprised, the pleasantries he offered upon seeing Ali appeared sincere. Still, Ali did not want to stay long at the home of a known Christian.

"I'm doing a study in seminary concerning what Muhammad said about the Bible." Ali had planned his words carefully. "Do you have one I can borrow?"

Jivan smiled at Ali's question. "Better than that." Jivan waved his hand toward Ali for emphasis. "I have one I'll give you. I keep extra Bibles on hand. It's not easy, you know, to get them in Iran these days."

Ali's journey into the Christian Scriptures began. His cover story if caught would be that he was finding mistakes in the Bible. Seminary teachers had told him errors abound in the Christian stories, and he wanted to see them for himself.

During each of the next six years, Ali read the Bible all the way through. He scrutinized the Gospels and taught himself to cross-reference and compare verses from the Old Testament with the New. He traced biblical themes and pieced together the fascinating realities of Christology and eschatology. The Scriptures captivated his mind and soul, but even more wonderful was the two-way communication with Jesus in his dreams. Ali asked questions about what he was learning, and Jesus answered. The two actually had conversations during the nighttime visits.

Ali wrapped up his official studies at Qom, but despite hours of surreptitious late-night Bible study and instructive and edifying dreams, he felt as if he had barely begun to plumb the depth and mysteries of Jesus. Senior clerics dubbed Ali a sheikh at graduation and sent him to Syria to begin his ascent as an area leader of Shia imams.

DOUBLE AGENT FOR CHRIST

In Syria, Jamal's conversion was as dramatic as any Muslim-turned-minister-of-the-gospel. His grandfather had been the fearsome Grand Mufti of the Gaza Strip, and during Jamal's Palestinian boyhood, his father served as a senior advisor to Yasser Arafat. Few families could boast more fanatic devotion to Islam than his. But Jamal's personal encounters with Jesus trumped his family background, and Jamal devoted himself to a very different faith.

Steeped in Islam and bolstered by his private experiences with Jesus, Jamal's skill in dialoging with Muslims netted numerous converts and sent many others on a deeper search for God's truth. He often appeared fearless in his witness. Friends had once seen him in a shouting match, defending Jesus' resurrection, with a testy, heavily armed Hezbollah soldier. Yet even Jamal was unnerved the day the region's upstart imam—newly imported and loudly trumpeted from Qom—knocked at his front door. Jamal feared the visit may be the beginning of the end of his flourishing evangelistic outreach to Muslims.

The two men eyed each other silently for several seconds. Ali spoke first: "May I come in?"

Jamal glanced quickly around the front yard and at the street in front of his house. Ali read the question in Jamal's eye movements. "Yes, I'm alone."

Jamal recognized that the significance of this visit—whatever it may be—called for diplomacy. "You are Imam Sheikh Ali?"

Ali offered a courteous smile and single nod in response.

"I am honored that you would come to my home. By all means, please come inside."

He held open the door for his visitor and then led him without speaking down the hall toward the living room. Jamal forced himself not to look back. If the man intended to kill him, it would be on the imam's conscience that he attacked Jamal from behind. As the host turned to offer his guest a seat, the sheikh reached beneath the outer layer of his robes. Had the imam shouted

"Allahu Akbar" and produced a dagger, Jamal would have been less surprised than what happened next.

The sheikh held a Bible in his right hand. He raised it an arm's length in the air and declared, "This book is the truth! I have been reading it privately for six years now." With corresponding flair, he pulled out a Qur'an with his other hand. "And this book is a fairy tale. It is make-believe like a Disney movie."

Jamal looked from the Bible to the Qur'an to Ali's face. He asked the only question he could think of at that instant: "Would you like coffee or tea?"

The imam requested coffee but refused a chair. Instead, the two men sat on the floor of Jamal's living room. For four hours Ali poured out the story of his parallel studies at Qom and his dreams of Jesus. Jamal chuckled at Ali's narrative about telling his roommate that he was having "nightmares" when the roommate would hear Ali cry out Jesus' name in his sleep. The imam explained his love for Jesus and how remarkable it was that the Man who met him in his dreams said the same things Ali would inevitably read in one of the Gospels the next day! That his dreams led him to the Bible had assured Ali he was still sane.

But Sheikh Ali had two serious questions and hoped Jamal could help. He wasn't sure about the Trinity, and he wanted a better understanding of justification.

"I Am Ready to Die with You"

Midway through their afternoon together, Ali's wife returned home. Panic flashed across her face when she recognized the man sitting with her husband in their living room. Understanding the reaction, Ali stood and thanked her for letting him spend such a long time with Jamal. She encouraged the men to sit again and talk even longer over a plate of cookies.

Jamal, too, had a question but wanted to make sure Ali had asked each of his first. In all the conversation, Jamal couldn't tell: had this man committed his life to the Lord?

As if in anticipation of what Jamal might ask, Ali fell silent, stood up, and looked Jamal in the eye. "I am ready to be a Jesus follower. I want to be a Christian. I know this will probably cost me my life, but I am willing to do this because this is all truth. I have been searching for this for years."

Jamal reached for Ali's hand. "God sent you here to influence all the imams of this area. It is no mistake. I will disciple you so you can become strong in your faith. You will need this when you go public because they will try to kill you. You are too valuable of an investment for them to just let you convert to Christianity without any consequences."

Ali nodded. Then Jamal added, "If they kill you, I am ready to die with you."

Jamal tightened his grip on Ali's hand. "Let's pray."

PART · IV

JORDAN—TOP HONORS IN HONOR KILLINGS

NINE

Clinically Impressed

J ordan enjoys a rich biblical and spiritual history, exceeded
only by Israel's. As a result, the Jordanian economy thrives
on tourism. The country's ancient city of Petra recently was
named one of the new Seven Wonders of the World. Often called
"Sweet Arabs" of the Middle East, Jordanians also enjoy a glowing
public image. Life is good in the Hashemite Kingdom. Or so it
seems.

Jordan hides a darker side never mentioned in tourism bro-
chures. The nation has the highest rate of "honor killings" in the
Middle East.

Middle Eastern society is built on the concepts of shame and
honor, and as we saw in Fatima's story earlier, Islamic families that
practice their religion must erase any trace of shame that comes
upon them, no matter the cost. This translates to social practices
inconceivable for most Westerners. If a young girl is raped, for
instance, she will likely become the victim of an honor killing to
rid the family of the dark cloud her violation has brought on them.
This will restore the family honor.

Even if a family takes a rape case to court and wins, the perceived shame still rests on the girl's relatives. They are all considered stained forever. This means the overwhelming majority of honor-killing victims are women and girls. And since Islamic society offers few rights for women, they are often *silent* victims.

While I visited the country in 2006, a Jordanian believer named Kamal told me the sad story of a young girl killed by her father for having premarital sex. He announced at a gathering that the sixteen-year-old would die that night for her promiscuity. After dinner, the father took his daughter to the backyard and, while her mother and siblings watched, drowned her in the family's swimming pool.

Reported to the police as an accident, the authorities investigated. When the father confessed to the murder, officials ordered an autopsy. It confirmed that the young girl was still a virgin.

After hearing the story, I asked the obvious question: "Is the father in prison for life?" Hardly. "He was released the next day after questioning," Kamal told me with his head down. "These are the things that happen in my country, and they are swept under the carpet."

In another incident, Noor was a fourteen-year-old tormented by her school bus driver. The fifty-eight-year-old man had made several attempts to lure her into a sexual relationship, yet when the girl begged her mother for help, she refused to believe the stories.

After repeated rejections by Noor, the driver saw an opportunity one afternoon at the end of the day's bus service. Noor had fallen asleep and missed her stop. The sensation of the bus engine shutting down woke her, and she noticed her classmates were gone. The bus sat in a deserted area far from home.

She startled as the driver appeared by her seat and pointed a gun at her face. He ordered Noor to take off all her clothes. Thinking quickly, the girl responded: "Okay, I'll take my clothes off. But I am shy, so would you turn your head while I undress?" As the older man complied, Noor grabbed the gun and shot him dead!

When I heard the story, my first thought was, *Well, he got what he deserved.* But that's not how it works in Jordan. And Noor, of course, did not get what she deserved.

Today she lives in a "shelter" for shamed women. Essentially a prison, the place has been her home since she was forced to flee her family—they had ordered her death. She also received a death threat from the family of the bus driver. Now she is protected in this undisclosed location, but she has no hope of ever being released.

It is extremely difficult to visit someone in a shelter like the one where Noor is exiled. The Jordanian government does its best to keep the existence of such places secret from the public. But people have heard stories and know that the shelters are real. A friend worked for months to arrange a visit with Noor, and when it was finally granted, the friend was shocked at the filthy, depressing world she entered. The life expectancy is pitifully short for anyone confined there. And young Noor's only crime was defending herself against a rapist old enough to be her grandfather.

So in Jordan, getting raped or being suspected of immorality or criminal activity will land women in a shelter. A woman can also get there simply by displeasing her husband in some way—like becoming a follower of Jesus. If a Muslim woman converts to

Christianity and is found out by an angry husband, she may have to live in a shelter for the rest of her life—if she's not killed first.

A 2011 article in the *Economist* underscores why conversion for women is so hazardous. It reported a shocking new poll from the Middle East in which Jordan ranked highest of any Muslim country. Eighty-five percent of Jordanians stated that if a Muslim leaves Islam, he or she should be killed.[1]

A statistic like that is especially frightening for someone like Jamilla. Her city produces the highest number of honor killings in all of Jordan.

TRIAGE IN THE SPIRIT

Hejaz Street. Jamilla's hope faded as she read the address on the advertisement for next week's opening of a free medical clinic. *Why would this poster be hanging in her mosque if the clinic is in the Christian end of Jerash?*

Gerasa, as Jamilla's hometown was called in New Testament days, claims a history as one of ten cities in the Roman Decapolis. Jesus visited this region, and the area is perhaps best remembered for the confrontation He had with a demon-possessed man in this dangerous area. In Mark 5:1–20, the Bible describes how Jesus set this man free from the "legion" of demons that inhabited him (v. 9).

The European dynasty that occupied much of the Middle East during Jesus' lifetime is long gone. But the ancient Roman presence broods over the area in the form of ruins that are among the largest ever unearthed in the region.

Jordan is an ancient intersection for the Silk Road of the Far

East and the famed King's Highway of the Old Testament, and the demographic diversity of Jerash remains visible today. Circassians from the Northern Caucasus live alongside Armenians who settled in the area to escape the genocide perpetrated by the Ottomans in 1915. While the various groups include Christians, an over-whelming majority of residents are Muslim. In the Arab Middle East, about 5 to 10 percent of any given population generally is Christian, but among Jamilla's Jordanian neighbors, less than half that number claims any allegiance to Jesus Christ.

Jamilla understood the problem her fellow Muslims cause for the few Christian residents of the town. The imam at her mosque had been known to send announcements booming from a loudspeaker on the minaret specifically to drown out preach-ers at gatherings in the closest non-Muslim communities. While there was usually little overt friction between the groups, Jamilla's neighborhood boasted a 100 percent "pure" Muslim pedigree, and residents were proud to keep it that way. The thought of mingling with infidels was repugnant—and most assumed the feeling was mutual.

Still, Jamilla's children needed help. *The Christians*, she thought, now staring blankly at the sign on the mosque wall, *certainly aren't there to serve Muslims. But I must try.*

ARE MUSLIMS ALLOWED HERE?

On the morning the clinic opened, the young Muslim mother walked into foreign territory with three of her eleven children. Jamilla cracked open the front door and peeked inside.

Three elderly men leaned wearily against a wall; several young women squatted near children seated on the floor, scribbling with crayons; a sickly twentyish single man hunkered in a corner; and a decrepit, obviously Muslim, older woman slumped forward in one of the few chairs in the crowded, makeshift medical clinic. The offer of free care was irresistible to the neglected poor of Jerash. Jamilla caught her breath at the already stale, overheated air in the waiting room. An older man and a child inside coughed simultaneously.

"Do you need some help?" a kind voice asked.

Jamilla sensed the words were directed at her. Embarrassed by the immediate attention, she stumbled on her response. "I didn't know if I should be here . . . if Muslims are allowed. May I come in?"

"Well, of course!" A young woman whose warm smile matched the cheerful voice waved her in.

"I have my children with me. Some of them."

"Wonderful. They're welcome too. I have something for them while you wait."

Jen, the medical coordinator for e3,[2] the US missions organization sponsoring the clinic, scraped several coloring books and a handful of crayons off the desk at her side and jockeyed through the crowd toward Jamilla.

The mother nodded thanks as she took the small gifts from Jen and motioned her children toward an open spot on the floor. The sister and two brothers sat respectfully, selected several crayons each from their mother, and began scrawling on the Arabic coloring books that told stories about Jesus. Jamilla smiled at their enthusiasm and then focused on the charming lady who had welcomed them so kindly.

Jen commanded the room like a New York traffic cop during rush hour. She recorded patient names and medical concerns on a clipboard, filed the information effortlessly, ducked into examining rooms minute by minute to check every doctor's progress, and gently directed each patient, in turn, toward a specified door. As Jamilla eyed the other patients, she slowly realized that *most* of them were Muslim. The observation mystified her but also put her at ease.

In less than thirty minutes, Jen had introduced Jamilla to a female physician from the American city of Atlanta. Dr. Lynn's warmth matched Jen's, and Jamilla overflowed with questions and concerns about the medical issues facing her family.

In the Middle East, many health problems are a result of cousins marrying. Although sociologists estimate that inbreeding is common among roughly 10 percent of the world's population, in some Middle Eastern countries the proportion reaches 50 percent. The practice is nearly unthinkable in the West, but in Arab nations, preserving a family line is paramount. The centuries-long history of tribalism has also encouraged inbreeding, particularly among Muslims. It is of inestimable value, for instance, to be a descendant of the Quraish tribe, the line of Muhammad himself. Jamilla, however, had not resorted to an intrafamily marriage. She was wedded to a longtime family friend, and Dr. Lynn confirmed that her children's asthma and allergies were likely not genetic anomalies but simply personal health quirks.

The weight of concern for her children lifted as Jamilla watched this talented physician examine the three youngsters. Dr. Lynn presented Jamilla with an inhaler for each child and suggested the devices might control asthma attacks well enough that no other treatment would be necessary. The doctor hugged each child, instructed Jamilla to bring her other children in for a checkup as soon as possible, and opened the door for her guests to return to the waiting room.

As Jamilla ushered her children out of the examination, she recognized a woman from her neighborhood. The other mother's eyes flitted away from Jamilla, back to the children with her.

Jamilla stepped close to her friend and whispered, "This is wonderful. Don't be embarrassed about coming here."

The woman looked at Jamilla with deep brown, tired eyes. "Mahmoud has been sick for two weeks." She raised a listless two-year-old from her lap to her shoulder.

"The American doctor is a woman, but she is very good. I'm sure she will know what to do for him."

"Nasreen." The woman looked in the direction of Jen's voice. "Dr. Lynn is ready to see your little boy now."

Nasreen glanced at Jamilla and nodded. She stood and carried the sick child through the open door of the examining room.

Jamilla smiled softly at Jen. "The Jesus in those coloring books healed people, didn't He? I've heard about that before."

The medical coordinator crossed the room. "Yes, He did, Jamilla. That's why we're here. To try to do the same thing."

The two women hugged. Then Jamilla prodded her children toward the clinic exit. As she stepped out the door, Jamilla turned her head toward Jen and mouthed the words, "Thank you."

VISITS FROM THE GREAT PHYSICIAN

The Man's eyes dazzled Jamilla. She stared as He stepped close and wrapped powerful arms around her shoulders. White folds from the arms of His robe draped her body. "Jamilla, they love you because I love you."

Another man's cough interrupted the dream, and Jamilla's eyes popped open. She lay in her bed, staring at the darkness, and felt her husband's weight shift beside her. What would he think if she told him of her dreams?

She replayed the encounter in her mind. It was the third time since her day at the clinic that Jesus had visited her. And it *was* a visit. On previous nights, He had talked to her like a friend, or perhaps more like a counselor. He explained things no one else could—or should—know about her. Her fears, mistakes, worries, selfishness, even her lusts. Yet the conversation seemed supremely safe with Him.

Jamilla wasn't sure how she had first known it was Jesus. Had He introduced Himself? No, not exactly. The first time they met, He just *assumed* she knew who He was. And that was enough. After that, there was no doubt. Jesus wanted to be her friend.

But a great prophet speaking to her in a dream, asking for friendship? What could it mean? And then tonight. He had never before said, "I love you." Somehow, He even knew how mystified she was by her experience at the clinic and wanted her to know more about the people there. She would have to do as Dr. Lynn had said and take her other children for a health exam.

PUSHED TO THE LIMIT

The medical team rose slowly to their feet in the guesthouse. Fifteen-hour shifts and examining as many as two hundred patients a day had brought the clinic volunteers to near exhaustion after the first week of ministering in Jerash. One by one, Jen, Dr. Lynn, and eight other clinic workers gathered in the common room to sip strong Arabic coffee. A breakfast of fried eggs, cheese, olives, hummus, and pita bread capped off the caffeine infusion, and the team was ready for their half-mile walk to the clinic building. They would make it there in time to spend thirty minutes praying, prepping equipment, and arranging office supplies before opening the doors at 8 a.m.

Suhad, the team's head nurse and only native Jordanian, jiggled her head from side to side, trying to see through the people already mobbing the streets for the day's activities. She thought she had seen an arm waving in their direction as the team approached the clinic. Suhad bumped past several women and stopped in the margin between the streaming crowd and the front of the clinic.

Jamilla stood by the door with five children. She nodded a greeting to Suhad, and as Jen stepped up behind the nurse, Jamilla reached for her arm.

"I must talk with you."

Jen sensed urgency, but saw excitement rather than fear on Jamilla's face.

"Jesus appeared to me last night—again! It was the third time!"

Jen glanced at Suhad, and then focused on the mother of eleven. "You're Jamilla, aren't you? You came to the clinic on the first day."

Jamilla nodded slowly, smiling that Jen remembered, and glanced over her shoulder to make sure no one was listening to their conversation.

"Yes, Jamilla. I would love to talk with you. I want to hear more about your visits from Jesus." Jen had heard of the increasing number of encounters between Muslims and Jesus but hadn't known of one firsthand. The thought that Jesus had come to see this lady thrilled the young medical worker.

Jen and Suhad ushered Jamilla into an examining room where she recounted her experiences with Jesus. Jamilla's children crowded in to hear the story as well.

"I felt His love, and I didn't want Him to leave. And He mentioned you—the clinic! He said you love me because He does. What does that mean?"

Jen picked up the question as Jamilla concluded her story. "Jesus has a plan for you, Jamilla. He led you here to the clinic so you could see His love through us, His followers. He wants you to be His follower too."

Jamilla's eyes roved from Jen to Suhad and back to Jen. "His follower?" She paused at the thought. "I have seen a television program and heard a radio preacher who spoke of such things. But I assumed they could not possibly mean that I, a Muslim, should follow Jesus."

"Muslims are killed for becoming Christian. My family would probably see to this. Their honor would be at stake. I even have relatives who are imams."

Suhad touched Jamilla's arm. "You are not alone. Many Muslims are meeting Jesus today. We know that this is very dangerous for you, and we don't underestimate the problems it may cause you. But Jesus chose to visit you, Jamilla. He is offering you His love and forgiveness. Jesus made all this happen—the announcement about the medical clinic posted at the mosque, your coming to the clinic, the doctors who could help you, then your dreams. They were all planned by Him. Jesus cares what happens to you."

"But why Jesus? Why me? I know He is a great prophet we

Muslims respect, but you seem to see Him differently. Why would He come to me like this? Why would I be so honored? I am just a mother. Why did Jesus not appear to my husband?"

"You have many questions, Jamilla," Suhad continued, "and I would, too, if Jesus appeared to me. But you have to remember that He did this because He loves you, and He is much more than just a prophet—even a great one."

Jen took the five children back to the waiting room and managed their visits to Dr. Lynn. While healing physical ailments was the job of the clinic team, healing souls was its primary calling and reason for being, so Suhad spent the morning answering Jamilla's questions and explaining the gospel.

Jamilla relished the freedom she felt in her soul during the talk with Suhad. "I have never felt love as powerful as when Jesus spoke to me. I do need Him. I need His forgiveness. I have worked all my life to please God. But this Jesus has changed my thinking. I may die for this, but I must follow Him. I must."

By lunchtime, Jamilla had knelt beside the examining table and become a Jesus follower.

The first visit to the clinic had lifted the mother's burden of worry over her children's health. This second time liberated her from the deeper weight of a dead soul. As she left the clinic that day, Jamilla wondered how she would explain this to her husband—or if she should.

FOLLOW-UP REPORT

The Jerash team continues daily ministry to Muslims in need of medical help. Often, patient encounters with the health-care workers are the culmination of several experiences with Jesus or other Christians. As a result, the team has seen as many as a dozen Muslims pray to receive Christ in a single week.

Jamilla remains a secret believer in one of the most dangerous countries to live in as a convert to Christianity. She attends an underground church and recently lost a friend there—the victim of an honor killing. To provide a measure of protection for church members, the congregation changes its meeting locations frequently.

Jamilla's husband suspects something about his wife, but he is not sure what has happened to make her so different. Jamilla hopes Jesus will work on him, too, but until He does, she keeps her faith to herself. For the moment, she is safe.

PRIVATE PRACTICE

At another clinic in Jordan, near misses with local authorities had reinforced the need for medical staff to be circumspect in sharing the gospel. Doctors, nurses, and therapists made sure their patients truly wanted to hear what they had to say about Jesus, and they usually talked one-on-one with people, to ensure total privacy.

Jack Mitchell, a physical therapist from Dallas, called in his first patient of the day. Hala had arrived before the clinic doors opened that morning and was at the head of the line. She filled out the required forms and introduced herself to Jack.

"I injured my shoulder last year." Hala placed her right hand on her hijab-draped left shoulder. "It still hurts almost constantly. Oh . . ." She motioned with her head behind her. "This is my husband, Abdul."

"I'm glad you came to see me." Jack loved his work and was genuinely glad each time he had an opportunity to help someone in pain. He walked behind his two guests, pulled the privacy curtain closed, and returned to face the Jordanian woman.

"What I'll want to do, Hala, is to help you loosen up the muscles that surround the shoulder. That should give you more range of motion."

Hala nodded, but a strange look in her eye made Jack pause before continuing. The patient leaned toward him and spoke quietly. "Are you a Christian, Mr. Jack?"

The smile dropped from the American's face. He had taken seriously the recent, renewed warnings against sharing his faith too readily. He also knew the area imams were not above sending spies into the clinic. Still, the woman had asked. He would not lie to anyone about his own commitment to Jesus.

"Well, yes. Yes I am."

Hala's eyes grinned before her lips did. Without speaking, she rolled up the left sleeve of her hijab. Jack's smile returned when he saw the tattoo of a cross on the woman's arm. "I love Jesus," she said.

The physical therapist glanced at Abdul, and the man nodded. "Me too."

Jack found out later that Hala and Abdul are gutsy local evangelists. They meet three times a week to disciple five other couples they have led to Christ. Every few weeks, Hala and Abdul invite other Muslim seekers to join them. They've discovered a question that, more often than not, puts their guests at ease and opens the door to fascinating and meaningful conversation. The new couples usually smile when Hala or Abdul asks, "Have you had any interesting dreams lately?"

TEN

Twice Converted

Too often, nothing politically meaningful gets done in the Middle East without someone—or many someones—getting killed. So when the late king of Jordan died, a witty believer in the Middle East told me: "King Hussein died a natural death. Which, in the Arab world, is a feat in itself."

Unlike many other rulers in the region, the Jordanian king didn't get his brains blown out. To the contrary, Jordan loved King Hussein.

Beginning his reign as a teenager, the monarch grew during his decades-long rulership into the elder statesman of the Middle East. His charming and engaging persona explains the affection people felt for him. The king was his own pilot, a scuba diver, and a motorcycle rider. He even married an American beauty. Educated at Princeton, Lisa Halaby became Queen Noor of Jordan. Noor al-Hussein—"the light of Hussein"—rejuvenated the heartbroken king after his previous wife died in a helicopter crash. Their fairy-tale romance and wedding was an Arabic version of the relationship between Grace Kelly and Prince Rainier of Monaco.

Jordanians of every stripe were infatuated with the king and his queen. Bedouins, the "natives" of Jordan, considered the king "one of them." Others gravitated to his simple, human warmth. He smiled continually, gave lavish gifts to the people, and showed up unexpectedly at restaurants to eat with the common folk— unheard-of acts for an Arab leader.

Even Israel admired its royal neighbor. His moderate Islamic beliefs helped King Hussein build bridges with the Israelis. He met with Israeli prime ministers for meetings that he kept secret from his counterparts in other Arab countries. Particularly fond of Israel's only female leader, Golda Meir, Hussein considered her a good friend. He offered a breath of fresh air to the Israelis, surrounded as they are by threatening Arab leaders. An Israeli friend once remarked, "If King Hussein ran for prime minister of Israel, he'd win easily."

King Hussein set the tone for modern-day Jordan, and his son, Abdullah, continues many of his father's policies. The result is a Hashemite Kingdom that offers a unique blend of ancient and new, cosmopolitan Middle East. In regional politics, Jordan remains moderate compared to its neighbors. The country even offers three open entry points along its border with Israel, and it has proven itself a good neighbor to others as well. At one point, more than one million Iraqis lived in Jordan after fleeing Baghdad and other deadly cities in Iraq.

The Hussein dynasty, along with Jordan's historical marvels, has fostered a thriving tourist industry. The Roman ruins of Jerash attract thousands of visitors. The Nabatean secret city of Petra is an architectural marvel. Hordes of visitors walk through a cleft in massive rock formations known as the *siq* (fissure) each day and trace the path that Indiana Jones rode in *The Last Crusade.*

The capital city of Amman is developing the infrastructure necessary to become a hub for regional and international business while maintaining old-world character in its colorful souks. Originally built on seven hills, the city now occupies nineteen, and the growth shows no signs of stopping.

One of the reasons Jordanians have the nickname "the sweet Arabs" is that they laugh often. Yet despite a positive relationship with the West (obvious by the number of Americans who travel there for Bible tours and sightseeing), certain older "traditions" such as Muslim exclusivism make life difficult for residents who stray too far from the common religion. In fact, the consequences can be deadly.

CHANGE FOR THE SAKE OF CHANGE

In Jordan, where changing religions can get you killed, Rashid has done it twice. Switching from Christianity to Islam was not such a problem. In fact, changing toward Islam is welcomed by most people and can even be a relief to the convert. Going back the other way, though, is another matter, and Rashid's story is a superb example of the mountainous challenges faced by a convert.

Rashid grew up in a nominally Christian home, but with respect to religious training in Jordan, it doesn't matter whether you're a Christian or a Muslim. Either way, you *will* learn a great deal about Islam. The religion and its trappings invade every atom of the culture. Schools devote chunks of each day to studying the

Qur'an and the Hadith. Although Christian children are no longer required to take Islamic education, opting out is like a tattoo on the forehead that makes normal socialization and success nearly impossible.

Rashid's struggles are best told in his own words:

> I went to church once a week, but I knew more about being a Muslim than being a Christian. The Islamic call to prayer happened five times a day, and we lived a few houses from a minaret. I also heard messages by the imam every Friday on prayer day. The amplifier was so loud that I could hear each word clearly without even being in the mosque.
>
> On the other hand, when it came to Christianity, I did not study the Bible nor was I encouraged to. My experience with the Christian faith was based on secondhand information given to me by church leaders. Like most "Christians" I knew, we celebrated various holidays, but it was just an excuse for overeating and drinking alcohol.
>
> Many of my friends were Muslim, and I knew plenty about their religion. Television shows taught Islam 24/7. I interacted with Islamic history and learned the belief system in detail by watching these programs. It became a part of me. In fact, if you had asked me as a teenager what religion I was, I would have thought about it for a moment and then told you I was Muslim. That's how little my "official" faith of Christianity meant to me.
>
> When I joined the military to defend my country, I developed a love for history. The Middle East was my particular passion. Jordan, I came to believe, is a special nation, and I was sure God had blessed us for a specific purpose. I relished

the knowledge of how we became a nation under the British Mandate in 1922 and then were officially recognized by the United Nations in 1946.

Our official national name "The Hashemite Kingdom of Jordan" made me proud. We are part of the Hashim clan, descended from the Quraish tribe that traces its ancestry directly to the prophet Muhammad. Along with my fellow Jordanians, this special distinction is what I cherished most.

In the army, I realized the importance of Jordan's connection to Islam. Even though I was not a Muslim, the heritage seemed so significant that I was slowly drawn into the religion. It represented my history and my people. Islam was the religion—and the Hashemites the family of my beloved King Hussein. Eventually, there seemed only one sensible thing to do: I converted.

My reasons, though, were not very spiritual. To me, Islam was not so much a religion as a cause that brought everything together in my life. I loved the way it made sense of my ethnic heritage and my military service. Once I became Muslim, my personal choice in religion made sense too. I was young, bold, and very proud to be Jordanian. And at last, I was no longer a minority in my own country. I was Muslim, and like my king, I could revel in being a full-fledged descendant of Muhammad. Life could not get any better.

I didn't care that my family was horrified over my conversion. I knew they would someday come around and see things the way I did. Christians were weak, Muslims were strong, and I was tired of mere religion.

I dove into the Qur'an, and the imam I studied under

considered me a prize student. I soon began doing the call to prayer in the morning . . . "There is no God but Allah, and Mohammad is his prophet!"

As I embraced my new religion, my Islamic belief system gravitated toward a strict, literal interpretation of Islam and the Qur'an. I became one of the young radicals, and the military was a perfect setting to nurture my emerging extremism.

I had no patience for anyone who did not want to fight for Jordan and for Islam. And I was pretty harsh about it. A lot of Muslims convert and just want to practice it privately, but I became a serious hard-liner. I wanted to be an example people would follow because of my zeal for the Qur'an.

Growing up as an Arab in Jordan, I had also been taught that Israel is the enemy. It may not have been the official public policy of King Hussein, but privately, many Jordanians harbored the centuries-old hatred of Jews. I learned it as a child, and serving in the army only intensified my feelings. The "Palestinian problem" spilled into my country, and that was another thing that made me detest Israel. I viewed the volatile situation with the Palestinians as Israel's fault. At one time, almost half of Jordan was Palestinian, so I figured "they" were "us," and the Israelis were the common enemy.

I was only a boy in 1970, but I remember Black September. The Palestinians threatened King Hussein's regime in Jordan—I assumed because of his good relations with Israel—and militant groups like the Palestine Liberation Organization (PLO) demanded to share in our government's power. War broke out that month when King Hussein decided to put an end to the Palestinian problem. He was probably justified since three hijackings had been engineered by Palestinian terrorists on the same day, September 7. One of the flights was a British airliner taken over in Bahrain and landed in Zarka, Jordan, just thirty miles from the capital city of Amman. It was an obvious attempt to make the king appear weak. The hijacker's goal was to force the king to pay special attention to the Palestinians. Well, he sure did. The hijackings happened right after several attempts on the king's life, and he was ticked. The captors off-loaded passengers and blew up the three planes, live for television cameras.

King Hussein declared martial law, and war began the next week. Although Black September lasted for one month, periodic battles between Jordan and Palestinian insurgents lasted for the next eleven years. That's when I first started getting interested in joining the army. Thousands died, most of them Palestinians. Yasser Arafat, the chairman of the PLO, claimed that twenty-five thousand Palestinians were killed, but other estimates say only about two thousand died. The armed conflict in Jordan lasted into July 1981.

Jordan survived, of course, and the king was restored to full control of the country. The Palestinian terrorists moved on, and Yasser Arafat was expelled to Lebanon. It was almost funny. After that, Lebanon expelled Arafat to Tunis, which expelled him to Gaza. He finally landed in Ramallah in the West Bank to keep causing trouble there.

My family endured the Palestinian War, but my conviction that the whole thing was ultimately Israel's fault made me want to destroy them.

I also did not trust America. They meddled too much

in foreign affairs, especially in the Middle East. Besides, they favored Israel and seemed to blame Arabs for everything.

After I finished my service in Jordan's army, I decided to go back to school so I could become a teacher of Islamic doctrine and history. But something very surprising happened to me in the process.

When I began to study the in-depth accounts of how Muhammad lived, it really troubled me. He went through fifteen different wives and probably had as many as nine at one time. What was that all about?

An even bigger problem for me was the responses I got when I wanted honest answers to my questions. I was not allowed to ask them. I sought out Islamic scholars, but they so got angry with me when I asked about Muhammad's life that I eventually gave up trying to satisfy my wonderings. It seemed that doubts just weren't allowed. But what bothered me most was the one set of rules for Muslims and a different set for Muhammad himself. I could not get over the inconsistencies. I finally asked one too many questions and was put in prison and beaten.

I was seriously disillusioned by that and slowly drifted away from Islam. More than anything, I guess I just gave up hope. The religion I had been ready to die for became one I wasn't even willing to live for anymore. So what did I do? I became an atheist.

Even though it seemed like the only realistic alternative to any religion, my atheist phase lasted just a year before God intervened. Unlike some people I know—one of whom I'll tell you about shortly—I didn't have any dreams or visitations from

Jesus, but God's presence became just as real as if I had. Let me explain.

Seeing my rejection of everything spiritual, my sister-in-law started to invite me to church—every week, in fact. She never gave up or got discouraged at my excuses and even anger at times. She just kept asking me to go to church with her.

The truth is, my main reason for not wanting to go was that I was afraid some other Muslim would see me coming out of the church. Finally, I struck a deal with my brother's persistent wife. I agreed to go one time if she promised never to ask again. She told me, "If you will go this Sunday, I promise never to bring it up again. You have my word."

Here's where the amazing God part comes in. That happened to be the Sunday the pastor preached on eternal security. The idea blew me away, and I was hooked. I even stayed after the service and asked questions. I had never heard of such a thing or considered that anything like it was remotely possible. But that pastor opened the Bible and answered every question. He seemed glad to do it too. The contrast to my Muslim mentors—if you can call them that—amazed me.

Before that month was out, I became a follower of Christ. My sister-in-law no longer had to coerce me into going to church. I couldn't believe it had taken me so long to come to Jesus. I fell in love with Him, the Bible, and telling others about the incredible Savior. The same pastor who had opened my eyes to the truth discipled me for two years. When he saw my enthusiasm for God, he suggested I go to seminary.

Sometimes I laugh at my strange journey from traditional Christian to Muslim to atheist to born-again believer. It's not a typical sequence of events, especially in the Middle East, but it was God's plan for me. I guess everyone's story is amazing in some way. These days, it almost seems more typical for Muslims to have a dramatic encounter with Jesus before they become His follower. I was blessed to have God use me to help one of them discover the meaning of his dreams.

SPEAKING OF JESUS

Ahmad wanted to talk with Rashid. But why would Rashid want to talk with Ahmad? The two men did not know each other well, and to ask for a meeting would seem strange. Rashid might even think it threatening. Their two families knew of one another but kept the distance typical of Muslims and Christians. Ahmad's family may be less well off than Rashid's, but at least they were Muslim. But Ahmad felt drawn to Rashid. He sensed something different about him, and he wanted to know more—especially now. He would explain that he wanted to discuss something "spiritual." When he called to make an appointment, his excuse worked. Rashid was, indeed, interested in such things.

Coffee steaming on the table between them and courteous words about each others' families exchanged, Ahmad studied the cup in front of him. The fingers of his right hand rested in the handle while he stroked the warm mug with his thumb. Then he looked straight at Rashid. "I am having dreams about Jesus. I want to know what they mean." He watched his companion's reaction as he continued, "How do I understand more? What do I do with this since I am Muslim?"

Rashid raised his eyebrows. "What does Jesus say to you when you have a dream about Him?"

"He tells me that He loves me and that I should believe that He is my way. What is 'my way'? What does He mean by that?"

"Jesus is the way to heaven, and He is merely telling you that you can trust Him to get you there. You cannot get to heaven through religion, Ahmad."

Ahmad glanced at the briefcase Rashid had brought with him. "Can I have a Bible to read about Jesus? I am sure you have one. I've been watching you for two years, and I know you're a Christian."

Rashid had hoped this would happen. He pulled out the Bible he had brought for Ahmad. "I keep an extra one with me. You may have this one."

Ahmad took the gift in both hands and looked at it for several seconds before speaking again. "What do I read in the Bible to help me understand about Jesus?'

"Read what His disciple John wrote. It's about Jesus' life. He explains things so you can understand it no matter what your spiritual background is."

"I am a committed Muslim, and I've read about Jesus in the Qur'an. Muhammad honored Him and talked about Jesus as a great prophet. So I know much about Him. The Qur'an and other Islamic writings even describe what He looked like. Have you read what they say?"

"I've read some of the writings and compared them to the Bible."

"What did you conclude?"

"Well, they were interesting, but I am not sure what to make of them. In one place, Sahih al-Bukhari claims that Jesus had curly hair, but later says He had long hair."

Ahmad ignored Rashid's observation. "Do I have to change my religion to follow Jesus?"

"I can't say exactly what will be required of you, Ahmad. It's probably best that you just start reading the Bible. See what you learn, and see if your dreams line up with what the Bible says about Jesus. The Bible explains the real truth, not your dreams. Many dreams are real, but some people have false ones. The Bible tells the difference."

"I will read John." He swirled the coffee in his cup. "Will you meet with me again next week for more talks? And please . . . do not tell anyone I have come to see you." He looked grimly at Rashid. "I think you understand why."

"Of course. This is between you and me."

The men finished their coffee and parted company at the door of the restaurant. Ahmad wrapped the Bible in a newspaper he had taken from the table next to theirs. For the moment, he was smiling.

THE FINE PRINT

Rashid recounts his next meeting with Ahmad:

Two days later, Ahmad knocked on my door again.

"I need a large print Bible," he told me. "My eyes are having trouble reading the small print."

I took Ahmad into my office, and when I turned my back to get a Bible off the shelf, something flew by my head. I whipped around, and Ahmad had jumped on the desk with a long screwdriver in his hand. He jumped on me, pinned me to the ground, and tried to stab the tool into my chest.

My family was upstairs, and they heard things being thrown around the room as I struggled to get him off me. I knocked the screwdriver away, so he grabbed the phone off my desk and bashed it into my head.

Thankfully, my brother had stopped by unexpectedly, and he raced downstairs. He grabbed Ahmad and held him away from me.

Ahmad cut me up pretty badly, but I felt the Spirit of God fill me with grace—and even love for the man who tried to kill me. In a way, I knew he couldn't help it, but I wondered what had happened since we met in the coffee shop.

When the police arrived, they took us both in and for questioning. I was shocked that Ahmad told the police everything, exactly as it had happened.

"He is trying to convert Muslims, so I was going to kill him," Ahmad confessed. "I do not deny it. You can take me to jail." They asked me for my version, but all I could do was to affirm Ahmad's story.

The Jordanian police don't mess around. They set our trial for the next morning. No lawyers, and no appeals either. Crime done on Monday, court case on Tuesday.

Ahmad confessed to everything again at the trial, and they sentenced him to four years in prison for attempted murder. When the judge finished reading the sentence, I asked if I could say a few words. The judge said I could but when I stood and looked at Ahmad, police officers grabbed my arms—and Ahmad's too—afraid that I might strike back at him.

I said, "Ahmad, Jesus died for my sins on the cross. He also died for yours. I want you to know that, as one of His followers, I am called to forgive others. And so I forgive you for trying to kill me. I will hold nothing against you or your family. I promise, too, that my family will hold nothing against you or your family. It is finished."

It was important for me to say this publicly because often the family carries out revenge to protect the one who has been wronged. I come from one of the largest tribes in Jordan, and it's a tribal thing. I wanted him to know that his family is safe.

I also told Ahmad, "I want you to know that I love you. I am going to come and visit you in prison."

I leaned forward and kissed him on both cheeks. He stared at me in shock. So did the judge and the police officers. One of them who I know is a good-hearted Muslim was wiping tears from his eyes. They took Ahmad away in handcuffs.

Afterword

Rashid reports from his prison visits that Ahmad is doing well: "I think Ahmad is going to be a follower of Jesus one day, but he is still puzzled as to why I have become his friend. When he comes to Christ, though, look out! We need his kind of passion—someone willing to die for what he believes. We'll probably end up serving Jesus together in Jordan someday."

The Great Awakening for Muslims

Today, we are in a showdown between the God of the Bible and the god of this world, and when we face off with Muslims, the confrontation is much like the one between Elijah and the prophets of Baal on Mount Carmel. It centers on the question of the ages: who is the true God?

Everyone who grasps the right answer will end up in heaven. Everyone else won't. The stakes are that high.

Scripture explains the scope of the conflict and who's involved: "We know that we are children of God, and that the whole world is under the control of the evil one" (1 John 5:19). While it may sound overwhelming to us to hear "the whole world is under the control of the evil one" (our enemy), God is up to the challenge. After all, the Bible says He can melt the earth with His voice—if and when He wants to (Psalm 46:6). When He moves a little bit, we feel the vibrations, and when He moves forcefully, the earth trembles.

From the beginning, God's desire has been that no one should die apart from Him. Yet a large chunk of His world has virtually no access to Him—no Bibles, no missionaries, and no one to tell them that God wants to rescue them. That's why He's been taking the matter into His own hands, as evidenced by the stories I share in this book.

GOD'S NEW APPROACH

I'm not a skeptic by nature. I'm actually known as being fairly trusting. But when I began hearing about Muslims having dreams and visions of Jesus, I must say I was quite the doubting Thomas. I think it's because I had watched a few Christian television programs.

People seemed to be having daily visions, mostly about things I really don't think matter very much to God. One woman announced that God gave her a vision of the curtains she was supposed to have in her new 10,000-square-foot home. For some reason, she didn't offer any Scripture references to back up her claim. Every time I heard someone talking about "dreams and visions" on TV, I found myself doubting his or her mental stability. I resigned myself to thinking, *God just doesn't work that way today.*

But I was really, really wrong. And did I mention that I was wrong? My good friend and coworker, Robert Hope, was the first to set me straight. He, too, had his doubts, but firsthand experience with Muslims opened his eyes. "Thankfully," he explained, "God showed me that my theology does not determine His actions."

After a few years of working in the Middle East, I found out for myself that God doesn't need me to tell Him what He can and cannot do in today's world. Just because some people wrongly imagine dreams and visions doesn't mean that God can't still use supernatural visitations today. God is happy to rescue people out of the darkness by means we more conservative types find unconventional.

About a decade ago, those of us who work in Muslim outreach started to hear about something new in the world of Islam. God was opening the closed hearts of Muslims by giving them spectacular dreams and visions. At first, the stories were rare, but today these amazing accounts of God breaking through to Muslims have become a common occurrence. We find that about one out of every three Muslim-background believers has had a dream or vision prior to their salvation experience. Some more precise surveys are a bit more conservative and suggest a little over 25 percent of Muslims had a dream or a vision before becoming disciples of Jesus. Either way, the percentage is significant. As powerful as dreams and visions are, though, they are just the door opener for most Muslims, the starting point for conversion to overcome the substantial obstacles between Muslims and Jesus.

OH GREAT OFFENDEE

Arabs are often strikingly gracious in relating to folks they don't know well. So while they work hard in conversation not to offend anyone, they do have a customary, somewhat courteous way out when they've had enough discussion.

In Arabic, there is a conversation-ending word that comes complete with hand motions. *Halas!* means "I don't want to talk about it anymore." Arabs say it with great passion, of course, wiping their hands as if washing them clean.

You're very likely to get a *halas* if you're sharing Christ with a Muslim and get the question, "Do you believe Jesus was the Son of God?" If you say, "Yes, Jesus is the Son of God," the conversation is *halas*. Islam teaches that Jesus was a great prophet, but that's as far as it goes. Although Muslims honor Jesus, and Muhammad spoke highly of Him, understanding Jesus as anything more than a prophet is a quantum leap most Muslims won't even consider.

This is one of two major obstacles for them. The second is the Bible itself. Let me explain more about how these truths cause problems for Muslims.

DUAL BARRIERS

In a conversation about heaven, Jesus told His disciples: "You know the way to the place where I am going." Thomas, the inquisitive disciple, blurted in response: "Lord, we don't know where you are going, so how can we know the way?" (John 14:4–5)

Jesus responded with these words: "I am the way and the truth and the life. No one comes to the Father except through me" (John 14:6).

In learning to share the gospel with others as a new believer, I learned that the Greek word for "way" can also be translated "road." Jesus' first-century followers knew this connection well because of the stupendous network of Roman roads that ran through Israel. The Via Maris or the "way of the sea" was the major thoroughfare through the Galilee area, and one of the stops along the route was Capernaum, where Jesus lived for most of His ministry.

Muslims can relate to Jesus' concept of a "road to heaven," but unfortunately there are two boulders in that road that they often have trouble getting around. Their objections are often put in these words:

- "You Christians worship three gods."
- "Your Bible has been corrupted."

It does not matter whether the person is a practicing Muslim or a secular one who has never taken his or her faith seriously. Muslims are taught these objections to Christianity from the time they are young children. One former Muslim imam once told me, "I was taught these two objections to Christianity when I was still in the crib."

I often reply to people who bring up the "corrupt Bible" objection, "Wow, the Bible is a huge book. You must have spent years reading it to come to that conclusion. And by the way, where are the mistakes?" I say it with a smile, and they realize I am playfully yanking their chain. They typically reply, "Well, no, I've never read it. But that's what the imam told me."

Objections to the Trinity are harder to explain to Muslims—in fact, they're hard to explain to Christians. But what I like to do is give a person a list of verses in which Jesus claims to be the Son of God and have him or her read them. Then I ask, "Well, what do you think He is saying? How would you interpret that?"

Usually the sheer power of reading the Word of God does something to the objection. People seem a little open to the possibility that Jesus is God and not just a prophet after reading directly from the Bible. But that doesn't always work. I do get my share of *halas* responses, and we end up talking about the weather instead. There are certain people, though, from whom I never hear *halas*.

GAME-CHANGER

When a Muslim comes to me after having dream or a vision, the two standard objections evaporate. I have yet to meet someone who, after having an experience with Jesus, is still hung up on the deity of Christ or the veracity of the Scriptures.

The Jesus experience cues Muslims that they have entered a new spiritual dimension. It rocks their world, so the pat objections instilled in them are replaced with a passion to know more about Jesus. Muslims may not know what it all means when they have an encounter with Christ, but they do know this: Jesus is more than just a prophet.

As exciting as these encounters are and as obvious as the effects are on reaching Muslims, we have to be careful to avoid presuming that we know exactly why God does what He does, unless it is spelled out clearly in the Word of God. So when I'm asked—as I often am—why God is using dreams and visions to open Muslims to the gospel, my answer is that I don't know for sure, but I have a few (hopefully educated) guesses:

1. The religion of Islam started with Muhammad having a dream, and every Muslim knows this. Therefore, dreams and visions are respected and are seen as a vehicle of divine revelation.

2. Islam is built on the concepts of honor and shame. These permeate the faith and often cause Muslims to do things that puzzle Westerners—like allowing their children to blow themselves up as suicide bombers. But for Palestinians, who believe their land was taken away from them, this is perfectly logical since the dishonor they feel has buried them in shame.

3. Steve, a Muslim-background believer (MBB) from the Gaza Strip, has a theory about the current state of Islam. He thinks Muslims are haunted by the continuing shame they feel over the rejection of Ishmael and the favoring of Isaac. Steve believes this is a major motivating factor in the "revenge theme" of Islam. The rejection of Ishmael resulted in a deep wound among Muslims. I encountered an example of Steve's theory in action on my first visit to Hebron.

A visitor to the Cave of the Patriarchs can enter from either the Jewish side or the Muslim side. Either way, you can see the Tomb of Abraham since both religions claim him. Once inside you'll also find Isaac buried right beside Abraham, but Ishmael is nowhere to be found.

The Muslim side—the one I went in—has an edge to it, though, because it is run by Waqf, the Islamic organization entrusted with the jurisdiction and upkeep of the holy site. The Waqf imams are rarely in a good mood. When I arrived at the tomb, I didn't help the atmosphere by asking one of the imams, "Where is Ishmael buried?" Oops. He shot back at me: "The great Prophet Abraham journeyed to Mecca with Ishmael and Ishmael died there, and that is where Abraham buried him."

In my studies of biblical history, I didn't remember ever hearing where Ishmael died, and I had been genuinely curious. I found the imam's story somewhat interesting since the Bible describes Abraham's burial in Hebron (Genesis 25:9), and both Isaac and Ishmael were present. But I decided I was probably over the limit for embarrassing questions with the imam that day, so I let it pass.

4. Muslims have felt shame and dishonor since the time of Muhammad, but they don't feel shame when Jesus appears to them. It's quite the opposite. They feel honored that Jesus would come to them. After a visit from Jesus, Muslims often say things like this:

- "I felt loved on a level like I have never experienced."
- "I felt safe and protected."
- "I have never felt such a surge of joy and peace."
- "I knew that He loved me, and I loved Him with my whole heart."

5. Muslims have a seriously bad image among the world's non-Muslims. Just about every night you can watch national news coverage of the latest terrorist attack, usually at the hands of "Islamic extremists." Muslims see these news reports, too, and know what the majority of the world thinks of them. But I think it's exactly in keeping with the character of God to reach out especially to those who seem hard to love or are the despised of society.

DO DREAMS REPLACE THE BIBLE?

I went to two great Bible schools, The Bible Institute of Los Angeles and Dallas Theological Seminary, and learned one of my favorite phrases about leading people: "Get 'em in the Word!" It's true. Studying the Bible develops a person's biblical worldview and staves off needless error, but the Muslim world has a problem on this point. Most Muslims can't read. Worldwide, in fact, Muslim illiteracy is about 80 percent.

Experienced missionaries recognize the obstacle this presents. George H. Martin is professor of christian missions and associate dean of the Billy Graham School of Missions, Evangelism and Church Growth at the Southern Baptist Theological Seminary. He also served in Southeast Asia as a missionary. In a 2004 article in *The Southern Baptist Journal of Theology*, he expands on the Muslim illiteracy issue:

> One correspondent wrote, "What we are finding with Muslim-Background Believers, MBBs, is that most of them come to the Father through a spiritual journey that covers 3–5 years.
>
> This pilgrimage often begins with dreams and visions, then the Father miraculously lays the Word in their hands and then brings a near-culture or in-culture believer to explain to them their dream/vision and what they have read. According to my almost 200 MBB interviews, the Bible figures centrally in over 90% of those conversions. In research terms this is awesome. It also has deep implications for the almost 80% of Muslims who do not read or write."[1]

Perhaps this also explains why more than 120 experiences of dreams or visions occur in the Old Testament. Through them, God could communicate freely to anyone regardless of whether or not he or she could read.

As I said, though, dreams are the start. In today's Muslim dream/vision phenomenon, the Bible plays a crucial part in completing a Muslim's understanding of who Jesus is and what salvation is all about. Of all the missionaries I have read or talked to personally:

- No one says a dream recipient goes to sleep a Muslim and wakes up a Christian.
- No one suggests that dreams are a superficial salvation experience in which the Muslim doesn't really understand what he or she is doing.
- No one claims that Muslims embrace these dreams and visions without understanding that Jesus died for their sins and that this requires they repent and follow Christ for life.

Here's what missionaries are saying:

- Typically the salvation experience is a process that takes time. While some take years, others come to Christ relatively quickly.
- The Bible is just as important in leading a Muslim to faith in Christ as it is when someone does not have a dream. Sometimes the salvation experience after a dream is actually more deeply grounded in the Word since the dream recipient has more heartfelt questions.

- Muslims who come to faith in Christ because of the explanation that they receive from the Bible possess a firm faith and not an un-Christian collection of beliefs. This is especially important as noted by a former Muslim imam who told me, "We have to ultimately make sure that Muslims become authentic followers of Jesus. If they believe a 'little bit of Christianity and a little bit of Islam,' that's just another religion. We call that 'Chrislam.'" It is not true biblical faith.

Today about 1.5 billion people are Muslim, and as we have seen in the last ten years, a significant number of them are willing to die for their faith. They believe Muhammad's words are from God and that Islam is the only way to heaven. But Islam, I believe, is the "final frontier" for Jesus' church. That's why He's taking such a dramatic role in leading the way.

PART · V

SYRIA—SPIES IN THE CHURCH

ELEVEN

The Secret Police's Best Customer, Part 1

T he portrait of Bashar Assad was new. Adel noted that it hadn't been there the previous evening—someone must have hung it up just this morning. Perhaps he would find out why tonight. It was the fifteenth day in a row he had been "invited" for a visit with the town's security officials.

"This is my body . . ." The church meeting in his home that evening had been sharing the Lord's Supper when the summons arrived. Every person in the group startled at the abrupt pounding on the apartment door. Adel Haddad's shoulders drooped as he set down the loaf of bread. He had hoped the whole day might pass without another command performance at the police station.

Adel stood in silence with his circle of friends for several seconds before he raised his eyebrows, mustered a smile, and quipped, "I am their best customer."

He kissed his wife and prayed a quick blessing over the two-month-old church. From his small apartment in the center of

Aleppo, Syria's largest city, the taxi delivered Adel to a lone building on a dusty road miles beyond the city limits.

This far out, Adel imagined, *the scenery probably hasn't changed much since the ancient days of the Silk Road.*

At least he could look around. His captors hadn't bothered with a blindfold this time since the night provided its own cover. Syria's obsessive control of its people is a model for other repressive Arab states. The police have so refined their internal spy network that some estimates suggest 40 percent of the population has direct links to at least one branch of the secret police. One of the other 60 percent, Adel's only tie is the periodic arrests he endures for leading a church. Despite well-heeled interrogation techniques, Adel has yet to help them expand the spy network among believers. Tonight he would be the guest of Shu'bat al Mukhabarat, the military secret police who report directly to President Bashar Assad and the main office in Damascus.

"Adel, is it true that you have Muslims in your churches?" the inquisition began.

"What do you mean by that?" Adel's face said nothing as he addressed his question to the official standing on the other side of the interrogation room table.

"Let me put it to you this way," Jabir Ramali squinted at Adel. "Are you baptizing Muslims?"

Adel had practiced his answers as well as his interviewers had practiced their questions. An uninitiated observer would have thought the look of astonishment on the detainee's face was genuine. Adel's eyes flitted across the large waist of the pudgy investigator, then his gaze locked onto his. "Am I baptizing Muslims?"

"Yes, that is the question." The large man breathed the words gravely.

"I assure you, Jabir, we baptize only Christians!" Adel did not look away.

The policeman stared blankly at his captive, missing the subtle evasion of Adel's answer. Realizing his response had won this round of discussion, Adel lowered his eyes to the table and squelched a smile.

Tough Times

Adel's path to becoming a leading client of the secret police began five years earlier. The nominal Islamic faith of his teenage years transformed into an obsessive drive as a young adult to discover truth about God wherever and however it may be found. For endless hours online, he studied every major religion in the world, convinced he would find an answer to his inner longings.

The beginning of the end of his search occurred the first night he met Jesus in a dream. The morning after, he tried to convince himself it was "only" a dream, a desire erupting from somewhere in his subconscious and motivated by his compulsive thinking about ultimate things. The next morning—the morning after his second dream—dismissing the experience was more difficult. Twenty-eight additional nights in a row of seeing Jesus left Adel helpless before the gracious God he had encountered. Within a week after the last dream, he found a Christian believer who could explain what he should do, and Adel accepted Jesus Christ into his life.

The intensity of Adel's search became the intensity of his commitment. He quickly caught the attention of the secret police and promised himself and God, even before his first interrogation, that he would always answer questions truthfully. But he wouldn't offer any information he didn't have to. Less than a year into his new way of life, he had his first chat with the police.

"Why do you hassle me each day?" Adel asked them. "Am I breaking the law by reading the Bible with friends?" He had tried taking the offensive with his questioners.

"You are if they are Muslims."

"Then I guess if Muhammad lived in Syria today, he would have to go to jail. He said in the Qur'an that the Bible was one of the Holy Books of Islam."

The interrogator bristled at Adel's waggish mention of the great prophet. "Yes, we know what the prophet taught, Adel, but Muhammad wasn't trying to convert people to Christianity."

The phrasing of the man's statement had destroyed Adel's confidence. He recalled the question his house guest Mahmoud had asked just a few hours earlier in his living room: "If I follow Jesus, am I converting?"

My apartment is bugged. A wave of nausea swept Adel at the thought. The four hours of questioning that followed blurred in the young man's mind, but somehow he satisfied his captors for the moment. Although they released him after that session, a detail of men in gray suits followed him daily from then on.

His next encounter with the police did not end as pleasantly. It ended in Bab Touma prison. It is the destination for Syria's "political prisoners"; the way is wide that leads to Bab Touma. Most any activity not approved by the watchers of Syrian society can be considered a political crime. For Adel, the crime was sharing the gospel with an Alawite. Alawites are members of the Assad family, and tempting them with an infidel religion is not a trifling offense. Adel feared he would live with the horrors of Bab Touma for rest of his life.

On the outskirts of Damascus, Bab Touma is known publicly as a maximum-security prison. By inmates, it is known as a torture chamber.

The screams of fellow prisoners were often harder for Adel to endure than his own agony. Pain, he discovered, became a gift that drove him closer to God than could have come any other way. A week into his Bab Touma ordeal, Adel thought his life was over, and he focused on becoming a faithful witness to the end. Although not quite a dream, he felt the "cloud of witnesses" cheering him on in the spirit.

Adel's resignation to life in Bab Touma freed him to share his faith openly with fellow prisoners and by default with the guards. Reciting psalms aloud, Adel periodically noticed one or more guards standing just outside his cell, listening. Guards inadvertently gave Adel a powerful opening to share the gospel with other inmates.

"Why," Adel would ask prisoners, "would guards who keep you here in the name of Islam and Allah, its only God, torture you until you are willing to shout 'Bashar Assad is God'? Who do they really serve here?" He exposed the sham of those who claimed devotion to Muhammad.

On his fortieth day at Bab Touma, when he felt as if he'd already been there several lifetimes, Adel was set free. He never knew exactly why.

TWELVE

The Secret Police's Best Customer, Part 2

A del's ongoing relationship with Syria's secret police has grown in him a perspective on the human side of their work that few people have. He's rarely angry or resentful of security people these days. God has given him a deep compassion for them that outsiders find remarkable, and he loves to talk about his "friends" in government service. You'll enjoy hearing how he tells their story.

TURNING THE TABLES

The Shu'bat [secret police] are human beings too. I know so many of them that I'm on a first-name basis with several. Being in the secret police means the government owns you. It's really a tough business. You go wherever they tell you to go, whenever they tell you to go there. But it's a job, and they're paid decently—enough to support their families anyway.

Many of them now apologize to me for the ridiculous

questions they have to ask over and over again, but they're just doing their jobs. I hold nothing against them.

My very favorite story, though, is about Mohammad. What an amazing work of God he represents!

Mohammad had been assigned to follow me and did a better-than-average job of it (I've gotten to know enough about how it works that I recognize who does it well and who doesn't). After keeping a discreet distance for several days, Mohammad stopped me on the street one day and asked a question no interrogator had ever thrown at me.

"Adel." He had a hard time looking me in the eye. "Why do you think I keep having dreams about Jesus?"

At first I didn't know if it was a sincere question or if he was trying to trap me. I've seen everything from faked dreams to faked conversions in Syria—anything to expose leaders of the growing house church movement.

But Mohammad was shaken, I could tell. In most of the encounters, he explained, Jesus asked him questions. Don't you just love how Jesus gets through to people? Mohammad was used to asking the questions, but now he was the one being interrogated. He did not know how to answer, of course.

The one question that haunted him the most was when Jesus asked, "Mohammad, why are you persecuting Me?"

When he got to that part of his story, he looked me in the eye and claimed, "Adel, I am not persecuting Jesus! I am just doing my job." He was really troubled by what Jesus had said.

I asked, "Mohammad, where were you when you had this dream?"

"In my hotel room in Damascus."

I told him that I know of someone else who had the same dream, and he was on his way to Damascus. That man's meeting with Jesus happened in the middle of the day. It was a vision, actually.

"Did this take place recently?" Mohammad asked me.

I couldn't help but smile when I told him it had happened about two thousand years ago. I don't think he was ready for that. He wanted to know more. So I met with Mohammad one-on-one—not in an interrogation room—for the next few months. A wonderful thing happened too: his dreams continued. The questions he came up with could fill a book, but he was a great student and studied the Bible with a passion I haven't seen in very many people.

Mohammad is now one of us. He's a secret follower in the secret police.

When he came to his first underground house-church meeting, it was an emotional time for all of us. Mohammad had put some of us in jail and harassed many of our family members in the previous few years. Some of the group could not even look at him when he first walked into our midnight fellowship meeting.

The tension was so thick I began by explaining, "We have a new believer with us tonight. Mohammad has given his heart to Jesus."

At first, no one said a word, but once they realized I was serious about Mohammad and his commitment to Jesus, the twenty people in the room shouted and praised God so loudly I was afraid neighbors in the adjoining apartments would discover what we were doing and call the police. Once everybody calmed down, we all laid hands on Mohammad and prayed for his family and for his safety.

Then Mohammad stood up and said, "Please forgive me for all I have done to you over the years. I have made your lives miserable by following you, questioning you, and threatening you. I apologize to you, brothers and sisters." We all wept many tears that night.

My mind flashed back to the time I spent in Bab Touma. That's where I first met Mohammad. He had been one of my interrogators—and now he was one of my disciples.

Later that night at the meeting, he told me something he'd never shared before. He said that the Word of God pierced his heart when I recited psalms in my cell. He was one of the prison officials who had been listening, just out of sight!

The day after Mohammad's first fellowship meeting, he was back on the job. One of his superiors must have told him to bring me in again since it had been a while. It was ironic that it happened the next day. It was also the funniest interrogation I'd ever had. Mohammad put on a great show.

"Okay, Adel, let's start from the top. What were you doing last night at midnight? Where were you?"

"I was with some friends."

"I bet you were." Mohammad winked at me as he continued the questions.

So if nothing else had convinced me, my experience with Mohammad taught why I should never back down from speaking about my Jesus. In fact, to help each other with that commitment, twenty underground leaders have now committed that we will take care of each others' families if any of us ever goes back to Bab Touma—or if we are martyred.

NEVER ALONE—A FOLLOW-UP VISIT WITH ADEL

Shortly before the writing of this book, Adel led a prayer team from America on a tour of Syria. Briefing the group upon its arrival, Adel explained that in Syria, you're never alone. The "suits" are everywhere, so he detailed carefully what could be talked about and what could not even be whispered during the week of the tour. When privacy allowed, he also kept the team apprised during the visit about exactly who was not a friend. These are some of the observations the Americans heard:

- "The van driver is secret police."
- "So is the waiter for our dinner at Damascus Gate Restaurant."
- "All three of our taxi drivers are secret police."
- "The boat driver that took us to Arwad Island from Tartous is secret police."
- "The front desk manager at the Semiramis Hotel and also the bellboy are secret police."
- "Our rooms are bugged."
- "Don't call home from your rooms."
- "All of the men in the lobby are secret police. When we go down there in the morning, they will all still be on the couches where we saw them when we came up for bed tonight."
- "Tomorrow, since we'll be in Damascus, there will be even more."

There is a "bright" side to the secret police, however. One prayer-team member wondered: "Why were all those men following us when we were shopping at Al-Hamidiyah? The souk was loaded with people, but these guys seemed to know exactly where we were going. What was that about?"

Again, Adel's expertise in handling the security force was clear. "It's for your protection," he explained. "The government is watching you, but they are also protecting you. The last thing they want is Americans getting hurt or killed in Syria. There are plenty of terrorist groups hanging around Damascus that would love to get a shot at you.

"The Al-Hamidiyah is tourist central since it's right next to the Citadel and the Umayyad Mosque. If something happened to you there, the international consequences for Syria could be disastrous. Besides the critical loss of tourist business an incident would cause, the Assad regime knows that if it ever falls, it will be the result of foreign intervention—retaliation for a terrorist massacre, for instance. Only outsiders could oust Assad because Syrian opposition groups are just not strong enough to topple his web of control over the people."

So for now, the web remains.

THIRTEEN

"Your Killers Are on the Way!"

H amdi is in a category of his own. Like the Roman centurion and the Ethiopian eunuch in Scripture, he is the first known believer among his people in this century. In missionary terms, he is part of an unreached people group. Growing up in an influential Alawite family, Hamdi never considered that he might find the truth about God outside his family's four walls. That is, until Jesus began visiting him.

THE ALAWITE DEATH-GRIP CONTROL OF SYRIA

Alawite history demonstrates why this people group is unique. One-time Muslims, the Alaween left Islam centuries ago and formed their own religion. Ever since, they've gotten varied reviews from other faiths. Sunni Muslims see them as apostates. Shia' Muslims regard them as brothers. Christians think they're a threat. And in Syria as a whole? They command respect.

The president, Bashar Assad, is an Alawite, and during the

2011 Arab Spring revolution, he threw the nation into a civil war. When youth protest marches in the streets turned into an attempt by the Sunnis to eliminate Assad, the dictator held nothing back. Syrian blood flooded the streets of Damascus, Homs, Tartous, and other major cities.

Bashar Assad employs a zero-tolerance policy toward civil unrest, a pattern inherited from his father Hafez Assad. In the 1980s, Bashar's father leveled the city of Hama and killed several thousand residents who challenged his authoritarian rule. And that was in just one weekend.

Because the Alawites are a minority in Syria, the Assads have created a sophisticated system to keep the population in check. The three branches of his secret police not only watch the people at large but they also spy on each other. And in the military, 70 percent of career soldiers are Alawite, including a strong majority of Syria's elite Republican Guard.

Sunnis often protest that they are denied many of the rights the Alawites have—and they are. But one freedom the Alawites do *not* have is the opportunity to leave their religion. If an Alawite commits his or her life to Christ, the favored status evaporates. Conversion is considered a crime against the government, a form of treason. So when a believer shares the gospel with an Alawite, even if the government doesn't retaliate, other Alawites will.

That's why Jesus took it upon Himself to meet with Hamdi.

ALAWITE DREAMER

Amir Salaam opened his front door and studied the unknown man standing outside. For several seconds neither spoke.

"Hello, Amir."

Amir scowled. Hearing his name from a stranger was not a good sign for a house church leader in Syria.

"My name is Hamdi. I must talk with you this moment."

Amir thought first of his family, gathered peacefully around the table inside, then of the commitment he'd made to God that he would share the gospel with anyone at any time he could. The man's demeanor did not communicate a threat.

"Well, certainly. Will you join us for dinner?"

Hamdi tapped his right toe nervously and glanced at his feet before looking at Amir. "Would it be all right with you if I just wait outside until you are finished with dinner? We could meet in private then?"

Amir began to understand. "No. You don't need to do that. I was just finishing. Please come into the living room, and we can meet right now."

Amir Salaam's expertise on the Alawite religion was well known among his friends—and evidently among a stranger or two as well. His burden to evangelize the Alaween had directed most of his life for the past five years. Yet so far, he had not seen a single believer from the Alawites. Amir had the passion, the knowledge, and the courage to share Jesus with Alawites, but he had not gotten past *halas* with even one of them.

Besides simply ending the conversation, Amir had found, the Alawites have a built-in defense mechanism against well-reasoned arguments for an alternative faith system. None of their doctrine is written down, so evasion is easy. All learning is passed through oral tradition, and they bear no trappings of their Islamic roots—no mosques, no prayers said five times a day ("that would be ritualism," he had been told)—although some Alawites "hide" among

153

Muslims by saying the prayers. Before Amir started his personal mission, he had been reminded by well-meaning advisors of the one hundred years of failed missions efforts among the Alawites in the nineteenth and twentieth centuries. Not a single Alawite church had been established. Yet Amir believed—felt somewhere deep in his soul—that God had a special purpose for the Alawites, and he wanted to be part of whatever that happened to be.

Hamdi thanked Amir for allowing him into the house, took the seat his host offered, and began an explanation of his visit: "I know you are a Christian. I am Alawite." Hamdi paused, gauging Amir's reaction. He could tell the man was not surprised. "My father is a sheikh and one of our major leaders. He schooled me well in the Alawite faith. I knew many secrets of our religion that others were not told since I was to follow in my father's footsteps."

Amir noted the *was* in Hamdi's statement.

"When it comes to Jesus, I know that John baptized Him and that is an Alawite holy day. So are Easter, Christmas, Pentecost, and Palm Sunday. We honor Jesus but do not worship Him."

Amir nodded as Hamdi hesitated, considering the words he would say next. He looked at the ceiling for several seconds, then focused on Amir.

"At first I had dreams only now and then—maybe once or twice a month. It went on for about a year. But then the Jesus visits began to intensify." Hamdi stopped.

"Did you have a dream about Jesus last night?" Amir guessed at what final straw had prompted this meeting.

Hamdi rubbed his lips with the fingertips of his right hand before answering. "Yes. Yes, I did. And I have had a Jesus dream every night for the last forty-five nights."

Fellowship and Danger

The Alawite church grew quickly after Hamdi's conversion. Amir and Hamdi agreed that once they had assembled a group of ten Alawite believers, they would hold their first communion service. When the time came, Hamdi, in honor of being the first Alawite convert in more than one hundred years, served the bread and wine. His hands shook as he offered the elements to each new believer: "This is His body! This is His blood!"

Hamdi's drive to share the truth that had changed his life fueled much of the church's growth. One evening at their home-church meeting, Amir preached, "A new regime won't fix Syria's problems. Only Jesus can do that. He is our great hope, and we must tell everyone this."

A soft voice speaking into a cell phone cut into his sermon. It was Hamdi. At the words "we must tell everyone," he had dialed a friend and told the man to come to the house and hear about a new plan for Syria. Minutes later, the friend arrived. Days later, he accepted Christ.

Saved by a Daytime Vision

The nature of Jesus' visits changed after Hamdi's conversion. Not all were at night. And at least one daytime vision saved his life.

Although Hamdi intentionally varied many patterns of his daily life, one essential part of his schedule had become dangerously predictable for someone whom so many people wanted dead. School ended at the same time each day, and each day, Hamdi was there to pick up his children. One critical afternoon, Jesus was there too.

Hamdi stopped in the hallway; he wasn't sure why. The notion had hit him several doors before arriving at the classroom where his three children would be waiting for him. Was he obeying an inner command?

A mother herding four children brushed past him on the way to the doors through which he had just entered the building. He scanned a row of grade-schoolers' artwork hung on the cinderblock wall beside him. As his eyes reached the drawing next to the closest classroom door, he flinched at a brilliant flash of light. The man he had come to know in his dreams stood in the opening to the schoolroom.

"Go, Hamdi! Your killers are on the way. There are five of them, and they are almost here. Go now!"

That was all Jesus said before He disappeared. A teacher stepped through the doorway at which Hamdi had been staring and aimed a questioning glance at him before turning and walking away down the hall. Hamdi shook his head, clearing his thoughts, then bolted past the teacher and into the room where his children sat.

"Come! Run with me. Now!" Hamdi grabbed the hands of the two youngest and motioned with his head toward the doorway that led outside through the opposite wall of the room.

The Alawite Christian and his three children charged down a side street behind the school as gunshots—originally intended for him but fired in frustration into the air—echoed from the front of the building. Four fugitives ran the half-mile to the home of a fellow believer, knowing it would be hours before his wife could safely come and take them home.

AFTERWORD

Hamdi's life has been threatened more than a dozen times since he came to faith in Jesus, but because of his conversion, the gospel has swept the Alawite community. Alawite churches worship in Syria, and several have spread into Turkey as well. For centuries, the Alawites have also passed down a rich musical tradition, and now that it has been applied to praising Jesus, they offer some of the world's most delightful worship songs.

PART · VI

IRAQ—IN THE BEGINNING, GOD CREATED IRAQ

FOURTEEN

The Swords of Baghdad, Part 1

Q uite arguably, Iraq can claim the longest recorded biblical history of any nation on earth. It's called the Cradle
of Civilization with good reason: the garden of Eden
was here. This was ancient Mesopotamia, which means "between
the rivers." The Euphrates River, first mentioned in Genesis 2 of
the Bible, is one of four major rivers flowing through the area, and
it still brings life to Iraq today. That may be why Saddam Hussein
built his palace right next to the river in this past century.

Consider a few of the other historical happenings that took
place in the country we now call Iraq:

- the Tower of Babel rebellion;
- Abraham was born in Ur (southern Iraq near the Persian
  Gulf);
- Rebekah came from a village near Haran;
- Jacob worked here twenty years to pay the dowry for his
  wife Rachel;

- Jonah preached in Nineveh and started what may be the greatest revival ever;
- the Northern Kingdom of Israel was captive here by the Assyrians, beginning in 722 BC;
- the Southern Kingdom of Judah spent its Babylonian captivity here, beginning in 586 BC;
- this is where Esther saved the Jews from an ancient holocaust.

During the Babylonian captivity, in the most significant Old Testament event for the Jews besides crossing the Red Sea, God raised up the faithful young Hebrew, Daniel, to become the ruler of the entire province after he interpreted King Nebuchadnezzar's dream. On top of that, Babylon is the second most often-named city in the Bible. The book of Revelation brings the story full circle from Genesis, and Babylon once again opposes God. Revelation 18:2 calls the city "a home for demons and a haunt for every evil spirit" (NIV 1984).

In the end, the Lord overthrows Babylon, and it is never seen again. Meanwhile, the surrounding country continues to generate its always fascinating, generally troubling history.

Two Faces of Iraq

"Muslim to the core" would be most Americans' notion of Iraq. But it hasn't always been so. Christianity has deep roots in Iraqi soil, although the history of the church in that country is not particularly glorious. Rather than missionaries or pioneers, the "settlers" of Christianity there were more like fugitives.

During the fifth century, a passionate preacher named Nestorius rose to the position of patriarch of Constantinople, the "governor" and head teacher of Christianity in that area (modern-day Turkey). While congregations may have enjoyed listening to sermons by Nestorius, his prominence brought him under the scrutiny of church leaders in other jurisdictions of the larger church of that day. Nestorius believed Jesus had "part of God's spirit" but not that He was fully divine. His influence so threatened the correct doctrine of Christ that the churchwide Council of Ephesus in 431 formally denounced Nestorius and his theological stance and removed him from his position in Constantinople. Although Nestorius himself was banished to Egypt, many of his followers moved east to Persia.

The area proved to be fertile ground for the cast-off clergy and their followers. Their version of the church became known as the Assyrian or Syriac Church and even sent missionaries back into the regions they had abandoned. Today, Assyrian Christians live in most Middle East countries, and although in 1976 the church officially rejected some Nestorian beliefs, its acceptance of the complete deity of Christ remains a matter of debate.

The Assyrian Church's weak view of Christ explains, at least in part, why Christianity fell apart in Persia when Islam swept in. Without a proper view of Jesus, the church anywhere is doomed to a mediocre existence. If Jesus, the head of the church, is weak, how can the church be anything but weak?

The most troubling aspect of this errant belief system in Iraq is the effect it has on individuals within the church. The understanding that Jesus is somewhat less than God leaves each Assyrian at a sharp disadvantage when faced with the overwhelming presence of Islam—that is, until he or she encounters the overwhelming presence of Jesus Himself.

STANDING UP TO SADDAM

Panic boiled onto the flat sand at both sides of the four-lane highway out of Kuwait. Yousef Samuel winced as a Hellfire missile shrieked overhead. He turned in the direction of the rocket's trajectory and gaped at tanks, trucks, buses—any motorized conveyance the retreating Iraqis could muster—spread more than thirty abreast across the roadway and into the sands. Any vehicle that got bogged down was either crushed by a retreating tank or vaporized by a warhead from an American helicopter.

The Hellfire missile that nearly ruptured Yousef's eardrums eviscerated a military truck, spewing pieces of its human cargo in all directions. Saddam Hussein's glorious occupation of Kuwait was ending on the desert floor along the highway from Kuwait City to Basra. How—or why—he had made it this far on foot Yousef could not fathom, although he was faring better than the soldiers in motorized targets along the road.

As two terrified infantrymen raced past, Yousef grabbed an arm and screamed, "Don't run! I believe God is with us!"

The soldier jerked his arm to free it from Yousef's grip, but as his angry eyes landed on Yousef's face, he stopped. This man holding him by the arm looked familiar.

Yousef had become known as the soldier to stand near in a firefight. The mystery of his survival during the war was so well-known that others positioned themselves near him, even sleeping on the floor next to his cot. Time after time, Allah or some providence spared his life. Missiles landing nearby killed or injured everyone in the platoon except Yousef. Murderous shootouts left scores of dead and wounded Iraqi soldiers, but Yousef, despite heroic performance on the lines, was untouched. He slept on a standard army cot while others took their rest in foxholes, yet he survived nighttime attacks unhurt. And now, even among this carnage the world would soon call the Highway of Death, he and his two companions survived. His commanders' plan to destroy Yousef had failed this ultimate opportunity.

Weeks ago, Yousef had proclaimed his disdain for the shame Saddam Hussein had brought on his country and declared his respect for the American enemies. As a result, he was among twenty-five dissenters sent to Basra, where they would certainly be killed on the front lines. Yet he felt *his* God—not the bloodthirsty Allah of most of his fellow soldiers—had spared his life for a reason. Someday he hoped he would know why.

DESPERATE SEARCH

Yousef's survival was only slightly less astounding than his personal introduction to the God who had assured his well-being. A nineteen-year-old living in Baghdad before the war, Yousef Samuel had maintained his family's tradition of attending liturgies at the modest but historically significant Cathedral of St. Mary. Home parish to the patriarch of the Assyrian Church, it was also the center of Yousef's nominal spiritual life. Not that he wanted a lukewarm religion, but the Nestorian roots of his church left Yousef with a foggy impression of the Jesus they honored on Sundays. Yousef did not know if there was any more to experiencing God than worship services and pride in a religious heritage that predated his Muslim neighbors' by more than six centuries, but he wanted very much to know.

"Who are You, God?" Yousef wailed in his parents' living room in the dim light of evening. "Do You care enough to want anything of me—if You're even there?" He repeated the questions he had cried at the empty house every time he was alone.

Yousef rested the back of his right hand across his forehead and let his body go limp on the couch. As his muscles relaxed, a thought drifted to mind, a reflection on the priest's words last Sunday about the need to be forgiven. *That's it*, thought the teenager, the clarity immediate. *This yearning. This hole in my spirit. I feel ashamed of my very being!*

"I need someone to forgive my sins!" Yousef shrieked the words in the only direction that seemed to make sense: up.

The young man lay staring at the painted surface over his head. He wasn't sure how long he had been watching the hole open in the ceiling before his mind registered what he was seeing. The flat surface eroded from a center point as if water had found a pinprick hole and gushed in, ripping the ceiling wider by the second. But there was no water. Instead, light sizzled at the receding edges of the cavity and *something* appeared behind the ceiling. Yousef's brain raced to process the impossible data flooding his consciousness. He assembled a face. The hole widened to expose the figure of a man. Although the body of the image hung above Yousef, parallel to his couch, the form appeared as if He were standing in place.

Jesus. Yousef could only think the name. His tongue froze to the roof of his mouth, prohibiting any intelligible sound from the young man. *You are Jesus. What do You want of me?*

In answer to his thoughts, the ceiling closed, ending his vision of the Man from heaven. Yousef heard a voice crying somewhere—not in anguish. Was it joy? Then silence enfolded him as the room went dark. He lay alone for many minutes feeling astonished . . . and forgiven.

Post-war Iraq found Yousef broke and jobless. Despite the sense of meaning his survival on the highway and the vision of Jesus had instilled in his heart, the young veteran was not sure what to do next. He had long sensed something lacking, even after the remarkable visitation, and wondered if it was the hazy purpose for his life that made him so uncertain. Yes, marrying had given him another reason to appreciate being alive, and serving in the army had bolstered his confidence that he could courageously commit himself to a cause. Yet what purpose could there be for anything beyond himself?

Magdy and Yousef had talked this over many times. His friend clearly thought Yousef's question was legitimate. He seemed equally clear that an answer would come. He was so sure Yousef wouldn't find the answer in Iraq, though, that the previous week Magdy had given Yousef one hundred dollars and told him to leave the country with his wife and go to Jordan. His one condition: "Before you go," Magdy had said, "I want to show you something in my home." This showing, whatever it was, was to take place tonight.

His generous companion met Yousef at the door. "Good to see you, my friend. I'm glad you were able to keep our appointment."

"I never miss appointments with men who give me large sums of money." Yousef smiled, took Magdy's shoulders, and kissed his friend's cheeks.

"I promised to show you something special." Two fingers on Magdy's right hand beckoned as the host turned toward the hallway and walked four paces. He stopped at a door on his left and pivoted toward Yousef. Magdy extended his right arm into the living room, silently instructing his friend to enter.

"They are not doing this just because we knew you were coming here tonight, Yousef."

Yousef's eyes locked on Magdy's face as he slowly traced the other man's steps to the doorway. The guest turned his head as if afraid of what he was about to see.

Yousef recognized Magdy's wife, mother, sister, and three children. The six people knelt at various points around the room. Magdy's wife opened her eyes and looked at Yousef, smiling, her elbows still resting on the upholstered chair by which she was kneeling.

Yousef greeted the woman with a half-smile and turned back to Magdy, who read the question in Yousef's eyes.

"They are praying for you." Magdy paused while the words registered with his friend. "We have felt led to do this for you for quite some time now, and we pray for you—here—every night at this time."

Yousef felt his face flush.

"We have prayed and know, Yousef, that God will meet you in Jordan. We have friends there you and Raina will stay with."

God didn't wait long to meet with Yousef. The friends took Yousef and Rania to church on their first day in Amman. Although the meandering worship style puzzled Yousef, the pastor's sermon did not. His message seemed crafted specifically for an Assyrian Christian like Yousef to whom Jesus was greater than the prophet Muhammad, for sure, but something quite less than the Almighty Himself. The pastor claimed by his sermon title and every word that followed that "Jesus is fully God and nothing less!"

God appeared to me. This new revelation about his vision years ago sent a thrill of joy through Yousef's body. Like the hole opening to reveal Jesus behind the ceiling above his parents' couch, Yousef felt his soul expanding to welcome this stunning new reality. As grand as the experience had been that day when he was nineteen, his understanding of the Christ who had appeared remained small.

That Sunday in the Jordanian church, Yousef realized he had perceived the man who had appeared to him as simply a messenger of some sort, more like an angel than the sovereign God of the universe. The thought of finding a specific purpose to do something dropped for the moment from Yousef's mind. Simply knowing this Wondrous Being was sufficient. Yousef had never made a specific decision to let this Person be special to him, but that day he and Rania committed themselves wholeheartedly to living for this "new" Jesus they now recognized as their Lord. From now on, nothing would matter more to Yousef than this. He felt in his soul that what he thought had been a great commitment to the army—and even the promise he'd made to his beloved wife—paled in comparison to what he offered the Savior and Lover of his soul.

Rania and Yousef stayed in Jordan for two years, first as disciples of other believers and then as teachers of Iraqis forced by the war to flee their homeland. Because of their joyful fellowship in Amman, the young couple from Baghdad felt as if they could stay in Jordan for years. Yet gradually the Spirit of the Man Yousef had seen in the ceiling nudged them in another direction—back toward home—and the gnawing desire for a purpose resumed. It was 2007, and they would be returning to what was statistically the world's most dangerous city for civilians.

FIFTEEN

The Swords of Baghdad, Part 2

S addam Hussein never lost a war. His titanic ego refused to note details of history like the annihilation of his army Yousef Samuel witnessed along the road to Basra. Or the eight-year catastrophe known as the Iran-Iraq War. At its end in 1988, observers assessed Iraq's outcome as, at best, a stalemate. Many say Iraq lost decisively. Instead of reacting to the outcome as if an Iraqi defeat had actually occurred, though, Saddam erected a memorial to the country's great victory over neighboring Iran.

Two enormous swords cross 130 feet over Baghdad's central parade grounds to create the Crossed Swords Monument. A legacy of the disgraced leader who personally sketched the original idea for the builder, it is also called the Arc of Triumph, hearkening to General Titus's more historically accurate version in Rome.

Several hundred Iranian army helmets, every one flaunting a bullet hole, surround the base of the swords, the placement of each earned by an Iraqi soldier who had gotten close enough to shoot an enemy in the head. But there were no helmets from his most recent enemies. The Americans had a way of winning not just violent public victories but gentle, private ones as well. One soldier from the United States showed an Iraqi the path to spiritual victory that would set him on a journey to help Yousef Samuel discover the purpose he longed for.

Together with three million other Iraqi Shiites, Hassan lived across the Tigris River from Baghdad, in Sadr City (the original, and current, name; the former president, in yet another tribute to his own ego, had renamed it Saddam City during his reign). Raised a radical Shiite, Hassan was happy to be among like-minded Muslims who earned for their side of the Tigris the nickname Revolution City because of their hatred of Saddam and the Sunnis. He was less happy, though, with hard-line beliefs that promised him only a lifetime of anger and violence. For the fundamentalists, he realized, Islam is more of an identity than a religion. For Hassan it was neither.

"Will this help me understand the dreams?" Hassan eyed the small book in his right hand and then looked into the face of the American soldier who had given it to him.

"Dreams?"

"The ones I have been having about Jesus. They happen regularly to me."

The leader of the platoon that patrolled Hassan's neighborhood smiled. "You've been dreaming about Jesus?"

"Yes. Every time I wake up from one of them, I feel a hope that I will soon come to understand why He would talk to me like that." Hassan glanced at the New Testament and held it toward the American. "Will this tell me what I need to know about Him? Will it explain more about this faith in Him you speak of at times?"

"You will be blessed when you read it, Hassan. And you'll see what a wonderful friend the Jesus in your dreams can be."

Lieutenant Clint, as Hassan had come to call him, explained quickly to the Iraqi how to become friends with Jesus, and the young Iraqi gladly accepted the invitation. He devoured the New Testament and became close friends with the Savior from his dreams. His encounter with God's love drove him to share his experience—some would say too boldly—with anyone he could.

Hassan was not content to wait for meetings that might happen in the course of a normal day. An urgency to introduce others to Jesus drove him to find a place where he could touch the largest number of people possible. That urgency drove him to Saddam's Victory Arch, the place where, handing out Bible tracts one day, he met another young man who was discreetly sharing Jesus with anyone who would listen.

Yousef Samuel stared, wondering if what he saw was another vision. A man stood twenty feet away, handing Scripture tracts to passersby. Sidestepping to make his way through the people streaming under the crossed swords (the Victory Arch), Yousef stopped beside Hassan, an arm's length from the man's right shoulder, and looked hard at the young man handing out pamphlets.

"What are you doing, my friend?"

Hassan's head snapped toward the voice, his eyes intense.

"Or perhaps I should have said, 'What are you doing, my *brother in Christ*?' Are you trying to get yourself killed?"

Hassan's face relaxed, relieved that this stranger was not an enemy. "I must tell as many people as I can about Him." Hassan pointed upward with his finger and eyes, past the arches. "Why don't you help me?" He smiled and nodded once toward Yousef.

The tract distributor's zeal was clear. Yet the military man in Yousef sensed someone operating more on instinct than knowledge. "Perhaps I *can* help you." Yousef nodded as he spoke. "And I'll start by buying you a cup of coffee."

As the two men sipped their warm drinks at a café near the arch, Hassan explained that Lieutenant Clint, the only Christian he'd ever known well enough to speak with, had been transferred out of Sadr City only a few days after giving Hassan the New Testament. He'd found a secret source for the tracts he was handing out but had been on his own with the Bible to learn more about this new relationship with Jesus.

While he was listening to Hassan's story, a plan formed in Yousef's mind, one that assured him he'd finally found the purpose for his return to Iraq, the reason for his years of training in Jordan, and now quite possibly the mission for his life. Yousef began to meet with Hassan daily and train him in his faith.

Hassan was the first of many. Trainees now reside throughout Iraq. They lead church in homes late at night, worshipping Jesus, praying, and memorizing the Bible. Most leaders of the underground church are careful about whom they share with and where, but discretion is a lesson Hassan has yet to learn.

AND NOW . . .

"Hassan has a particular burden for Shiite families," Yousef recounts. "He can see they are passionate for Islam and are committed wholeheartedly. He said his heart breaks for them. He wanted to reach every Shiite, but people were getting suspicious, and his life was already in danger. So I told him to just walk through his neighborhood—quietly!—and touch as many homes as he could while praying."

From discreet daily prayers for the people of Sadr City, Hassan moved once again in more brazen directions for sharing his faith. Most recently, he has specialized in ministering to Shiites during Ashura. The annual observance in Karbala of the death of the founder of Shia Islam and grandson of Muhammad, Husain Ali, Ashura is a violent and morbid display of religious fervor.

Processions swarm the streets, wailing and moaning in grief. Shiite leaders offer laborious speeches about the greatness of Ali and what could have been if he was recognized as the leader of Islam. Men brandish whips and chains and beat themselves until they bleed. It is the physical manifestation of the spiritual war that rages unseen.

Hassan battles in prayer and proclamation of the truth about Jesus in the midst of this crushing darkness every year, sometimes fighting spiritually induced physical sickness to fulfill his calling. He holds nothing back when he shares Jesus—which means he really should be a dead man by now.

PART · VII

ISRAEL, GAZA, AND THE WEST BANK—WALLS STILL COME DOWN

SIXTEEN

Will the Real Jesus Please Stand Up?

I n the Middle East, there are three ancient faiths: Judaism, Christianity, and Islam. I'd like to give you my one-word summary of each and explain why.

Judaism—Knowledge

The word for Judaism is knowledge. If you go to the Western Wall in Jerusalem, you will find Orthodox Jews there, praying. You will also find them studying. Right next to the men's section of the Wall is the Scriptorium, where rabbis and scholars continue the honorable legacy of studying the Torah and Mishnah. Mishnah is also called the "Oral Torah," and the word can be translated "to study, review" or "repetition."

While secular Jews do not spend much time with the holy books, they study other subjects and excel in most. Jews have won about 20 percent of all Nobel Peace Prizes even though they comprise only 0.2 percent of the world's population.[1] That means they've won roughly 110 times their fair share of the awards.

This passion for study trickles down to daily life, as one Jewish woman reminded me. "Typical American mothers say to their children, 'Don't forget your lunch,'" she pointed out. "But Jewish mothers say to their children, 'Don't forget your books!'" Whether or not a Jew is religious, knowledge is at the top of the personal values list.

ISLAM—POWER

For Islam, the word I would offer is *power*. Land represents power and is extremely important, especially if it has been lost through wars (or peace treaties). The struggle for power is the reason for the Sunni-Shiite fault line. The two sides rarely come together—except for their ultimate power struggle against the Jews—and several years ago, I saw firsthand how frightful this division among Muslims can be.

There are times when the "Little Town of Bethlehem" does not lie so very still. I happened to be in town on one such occasion. I was walking down Nativity Street when a ten-car motorcade raced up to the crowds coming out of the Church of the Nativity.

Palestinian men who looked like bouncers from Caesar's Palace pointed automatic weapons out the windows, inches from our faces, and scanned the crowds for Hamas infiltrators. Everyone froze. I was sipping a Diet Pepsi at the time, and I remember thinking that if it slipped out of my hand, I would probably look like Swiss cheese in about two seconds.

But why the fuss? Because Hamas terrorists were rumored to

be in Bethlehem, and at that point, the two Palestinian groups hated each other. The Hamas were itching to blow the Fatah meeting to smithereens. Today, Hamas and Fatah have banded together so they can have more *power* against the Jewish state. Whether Muslim groups are fighting Jews, Americans, or each other, it's all about power.

CHRISTIANITY—LOVE

When it comes to followers of Christ, the word that should jump out to all of us is love. Jesus performed the ultimate act of love with his sacrifice on the cross.

He washed the disciples' dirty feet; then He told them something you probably have memorized: "By this everyone will know that you are my disciples, if you love one another" (John 13:35).

People long to see someone living this way for Jesus. The number one reason Muslims come to faith in Christ is because of love. In surveys of Muslim-background believers, the love they see between believers and the love offered to them topped the list of reasons they became Jesus followers. It's not just the dream thing. Whether reaching out to a Muslim or a Jew, love makes the crucial difference.

IN SEARCH OF THE REAL JESUS

Often in sharing Christ with Muslims (and central to the story I'm about to tell), a make-or-break question arises: Is the Jesus of the Qur'an the same as the Jesus of the Bible? Although American

Christians may be tempted to offer a quick, potentially shallow answer, Muslims have good reason to ask.

In some Koranic suras, Jesus is presented fairly and accurately, but in others there are contradictory statements. Jeff Morton's excellent book on the subject, *Two Messiahs—The Jesus of Christianity and the Jesus of Islam*, offers an outstanding summary (excerpted below) of the issues involved on this point.

Qur'anic Statements about Jesus[2] Backed by the Bible:

- He was born of a virgin.
- He was the Son of Mary.
- He had the power to perform miracles.
- He was called the Messiah.
- He was given revelation.
- He had disciples.

Qur'anic Statements about Jesus Not Backed by the Bible:

- He was only human and had no divine nature. (4:171)
- He was a created being and not the Word of God. (4:171)
- He was a messenger for Israel only and not the Light of the World. (3:49–51)
- He was raised to Allah rather than died on a cross. (3:55)
- He was a Muslim. (42:13)
- He is not equal with Allah. It is blasphemy to say He is equal with God. (5:17)
- He spoke from the cradle. (3:46)

What's Missing in the Qur'an?

- Jesus' connection to the temple, the Torah, and the kingdom of God. These are not mentioned even once.
- Jesus' messages that address reconciliation, forgiveness, restoration, covenant, and many other major Bible themes.
- Jesus speaking of God as His Father.
- He is not called Immanuel, the Lamb of God, Son of God, Son of Man, or other biblical names for the Messiah.
- Jesus neither died on the cross nor rose from the dead.

So, when talking to Muslims, Christians are not dealing with a clean slate. Muslims have built-in presuppositions difficult to overcome, but if we don't address these issues we risk presenting a false Jesus.

ZACCHAEUS HE'S NOT!

Archaeologists claim that Jericho is home to the oldest building ever unearthed. It's one of the prizes of the Holy Land, and some prize events happened there too. Likely the first that comes to mind is Joshua's conquest of the city. To grab it for the Israelites, all he had to do was listen to God, command the people to follow the plan, and carry it out. Walls collapsed. Soldiers rushed in. City captured.

More than a millennium later, walls of a different sort fell in the heart of a Jericho man when Jesus came to town. Unashamed of his short stature, he didn't seem at all embarrassed to climb a tree so he could get a glimpse of Jesus. And until Jesus stopped under Zach's tree, the tax collector was not particularly ashamed of his scum-of-the-earth profession either. Jesus shocked the Pharisees— probably for about the tenth time that day—by having lunch at the tax man's house, and the outcast repented.

With that story in mind, I headed into Jericho in March 2011 with my wife, my friend Arthur Blessitt, and his wife, Denise. Arthur holds a place in the Guinness Book of World Records for carrying his eight-foot cross through every nation in the world. Imagine carrying it through Iran, Pakistan, or Saudi Arabia, and you'll realize Arthur is no stranger to conflict. So we headed into the West Bank with the cross in tow.

We told Israeli Defense Force soldiers that we wanted to retrace the path of Jesus, Mary, and Joseph as they fled Israel from King Herod, and their journey went right through Gaza. Our explanation went over about as well as a ham sandwich at a Jewish wedding, but to my surprise, we walked through Ramallah and discovered that most Muslims appreciated our plan and even welcomed the cross. It certainly beat the shots I had expected to hear fired into the air hoping to drive us off. Even Jericho was welcoming—at first.

Enjoying the gracious hospitality Arabs are famous for, we cruised the streets of the ancient city, lugging the cross. We received smiles, got the thumbs-up sign, and the women in our group hugged many sweet Muslim ladies and took pictures with them all along our path.

One young man, though, was not so ecstatic about our presence. The twenty-eight-year-old dressed in traditional Islamic clothing wasn't especially tall, yet he didn't offer anything near a Zacchaeus-type welcome. The scowl on his face as we passed his shop would have intimidated a special-ops fighter. As I wondered if I was about to see steam coming out of his ears, he glared directly at me and shouted.

"If Jesus is so powerful, Mr. Christian, then how come He couldn't even get Himself down from the cross? Answer that one for me, and I'll become a Christian!"

Nimer thought he'd sink me with his opening salvo, but I couldn't believe the overt opportunity I'd been handed.

"Is that a promise?" I smiled, genuinely.

"Are you trying to make fun of me?" Nimer shot back.

The man was not only mad at us for hauling a cross through an Islamic city, but now I had offended him personally. Perhaps I hadn't handled my conversation opener so well after all.

What I wouldn't have given just then for a moment or two of perfect recall. Nimer's seething rebuke threw me off. The second or two I paused seemed like an hour, but the Spirit of God came to my rescue.

"Nimer," I began, "that's an easy one." (What a stretch!) "Jesus was born to go to that cross. He didn't get tacked up there against His will. He even told everybody, 'I lay down my life. . . . No one takes it from me, but I lay it down of my own accord.' It's right in the Bible, John 10:17 and 18."

"That's the dumbest thing I've ever heard in my life!" (Remember what I said about Muslims and power? Nimer wasn't impressed with Jesus' strategy.) "Some kind of God Jesus is!" Nimer turned his back and stormed into his shop, muttering something about weakness and Christians.

THE WRONG JESUS

Nimer knew all about Jesus. It was just the wrong one. He had studied the Jesus of the Qur'an, and that one didn't die on the cross. In my exchange with Nimer, I had merely reinforced his bias that "The Bible has been corrupted." Behind his taunting, Nimer was telling me, "I know about Jesus, but yours isn't the one I learned about in the Qur'an."

In his book *The Two Messiahs*, Jeff Morton explains how this problem develops:

> There was no reason to try to understand what Jesus looked like—unless of course he was made to look like Muhammad. In fact, it is most likely that the portrayals of all the biblical prophets were built on the character of Muhammad. Muhammad stands as the template for each previous prophet. As the final messenger, a prophet magna cum laude, he sums up all the previous voices of God. What we find in the Qur'an are many deliberate comparisons of the biblical prophets with Muhammad. It is as if the life of Muhammad is being read back into the lives of the biblical prophets.[3]

Nimer was ready to break me in half because he saw Muhammad up there on the cross. Since Muhammad was a warrior, he wouldn't have stayed on the cross for two minutes. But Rollo May explains why Jesus' method was the only way to salvation:

> If Christ had been too proud to die, he could not have helped us whose basic sin is pride. So Paul and others argue that by

giving himself up without pride, Christ makes up for Adam's sin of arrogance.[4]

Nimer, of course, will probably never read Rollo May's argument, and if he did, it probably wouldn't change the way he thinks. Reasoning alone generally doesn't convince Muslims, unless something else happens first. That's why I found someone who could give me Nimer's e-mail address, and I sent my friend in Jericho this message: "Praying for you, Nimer. Let me know if you have any interesting dreams. See you next time I'm in Jericho."

SEVENTEEN

"I Hate the Jews!"

Habib's hatred of the Jews matched that felt by his Muslim neighbors. After all, living in Bethlehem was just as hard on Christians as on Muslims. He, his family, and friends used to drive into Jerusalem two or three times a week, but now just the process of obtaining permission to go there can take a month. Six miles from the heart of Bethlehem to the Old City, and it might as well be in another country.

It is another country, Habib thought as he stared across the Hinnom Valley from the balcony of his miniscule apartment. *That cement barrier across the edge of town makes me nauseous. It has wrecked everyone's lives.*

Habib obsessed about the wall. When the Israelis built it to keep Palestinians like him in, or out—he wasn't sure which—"business as usual" ceased. It became a twenty-six-foot-high symbol of the control the power-hungry Jews held over the town in which his family had lived for generations. He would have joined Hamas if only to have a chance someday to bomb a hole in the barrier, but of course, the organization would not have anyone from a Christian family. Never mind that he would just as soon call himself a Muslim.

The "evangelical" Christians he knew were almost as hate-worthy as the Jews themselves. Habib regarded them as sell-outs, compromising their integrity as Palestinians just so they could claim a few converts to their way of thinking. He was pleased with himself when he hit upon a creative means of undermining the cowardly evangelical lifestyle. He networked a handful of friends to monitor the church people's plans. Whenever they baptized new believers, Habib called West Bank Islamic leaders and reported that the Christians were converting Muslims. The inquiries that followed kept the evangelicals preoccupied for days.

Worst among the local filth were Israeli soldiers—especially the ones on duty at the wall. They were enforcers of the evil occupation, the bull's-eye on the dartboard of Palestinian radicals.

For a while after the wall went up, Habib nurtured his hateful outlook on all "the others." Within a handful of months, though, he had learned the new travel system and kept his paperwork in good order. His experience after repeated trips through the checkpoint now left him troubled. His disquiet centered on one particular Israeli Defense Force soldier. The man simply would not fit the only mold in Habib's mind for Israeli military personnel. This one was—there seemed no other way to put it—nice. He even had a name: Danny.

Danny gave the impression of sincerity each time he asked Habib about his family. Habib had even heard Danny the guard sound as courteous to rude people as if he were Danny the guide. But Habib told no one about his growing fondness for the intriguing man at the wall—until the day Danny saved Habib's life.

SAVED BY THE WALL

The shotgun blast ripped a hole in Habib's stomach. In the instant before his body slammed to the floor of his bedroom, thoughts convulsed his shocked brain. *How did that happen? Now I'll miss the dove hunt tomorrow morning! I never leave my gun loaded!*

Two parents burst into Habib's room, panic and horror blending at the sight of their son bleeding to death on the floor.

"They'll never be able to save me at the clinic!" Habib spewed the words at his father and mother. "Take me to the checkpoint!"

Through wavering consciousness, Habib could tell from the look on his father's face that the man thought his son had lost his mind.

"Take me!"

"Oh, God, help!" His mother bawled as Habib's father struggled to lift his dying son.

Aware of little else but stunning pain in his midsection, Habib joined his mother in prayer, but it was much more specific than his mother's request: "Please, God, let Danny be on duty when we get there!"

Habib's father disciplined himself to slow the car before approaching the wall. A vehicle speeding toward the checkpoint would alarm the soldiers on duty and—at best—delay their passage through.

Despite fear for his son's life, Habib's father noted the pleasant expression on the face of the uniformed man who approached the car. "He's the one," Habib rasped from the backseat. He had labored to raise himself on an elbow to see who would meet them.

Danny recognized the car and stooped to look in the driver's window. Habib saw the color drain from Danny's face as he peered at Habib and comprehended the gravity of his friend's condition. The soldier opened the back door and crouched close to the wounded man's head.

"Habib, don't tell anyone this." He pulled a card from his vest pocket. "You have to take my military ID and head straight to Hadassah Hospital on Mount Scopus. You and I are about the same size and look similar, so they won't ask questions. You have to do this."

Habib grabbed the hand holding the soldier's identification. "You'll be dismissed from the IDF and disgraced for doing this, Danny."

"It doesn't matter. Just go, my friend."

Minutes later, surgeons at Hadassah Hospital believed they were operating on an Israeli soldier who was a victim of an accidental shooting. Only when the real owner of the ID showed up the next morning to visit their patient did details of the story begin to circulate.

Habib's hatred of Jews was undermined further when, far from disgracing Danny, the Israeli government branded him a hero because of his sacrifice and commitment to peace. And perhaps most troubling of all to his long-standing attitude, the medical staff continued their kindness and humane treatment even when they found out Habib was Palestinian.

Throughout weeks of recovery, one question dominated Habib's thoughts: *Why would God save me from certain death?* Surely it was not so he could join a militant group like Hamas and fight to destroy Israel.

The question wandered through his mind as he drifted to

sleep one night during his third week in the hospital. When a light flashed from the doorway of his room, he assumed one of the nurses was making her rounds. But then Habib realized the place he lay was not the hospital room in which he had gone to sleep, and the light was coming from . . . a man. Something profound passed between them as the person spoke four words: "I love you, Habib."

Habib awoke to his room at the medical center and knew the man in his dream had been Jesus. Spurred by several recurrences of the same visitation, Habib found a Bible and read the New Testament all the way through the next week.

Now Habib had a new question: *How have I missed Jesus all this time?* It seemed especially ironic given that he and his newfound Savior were born in the same town.

FULL RECOVERY

Today Habib has embraced Christ completely. And Danny?

"Danny is like a brother to me," says Habib. "I've been threatened because of our friendship, and I finally had to leave the West Bank. All because I am friends with a Jew who saved my life."

Habib has also joined forces with people quite different from the Hamas combatants who attracted him before his conversion. Part of the Reconciliation Movement of Jews and Palestinians, Habib now risks his life to bring down walls not made of concrete.

———————————————

EIGHTEEN

Hummus with Hamas

I visited the Gaza area for the first time just a few months after
the September 11, 2001, attack on America. That may seem
like bad timing, but in Gaza City a Muslim woman opened
my eyes to the heart and plight of the people there. She recognized
me as an American and stopped me on the street. Reaching from
under her traditional hijab, she gripped my arm. "Did you see on
CNN the people cheering in Gaza when the buildings fell to the
ground and so many Americans died?"

I had, in fact, seen that video.

"Well, I wasn't cheering," she continued as if seeking some sort
of forgiveness. "I was crying for those people and their families.
Because that was wrong and they didn't deserve to die."

I thanked her and walked on. I also thanked God for the
encounter. Yes, there are thirteen known terrorists groups holed
up in Gaza, but there are also human beings whose inner conflict
mirrors the outer conflict around them.

Subsequent visits to Gaza have netted a friendship that has
deepened my appreciation of the problems to which that woman

on the street first introduced me. The more I get to know this particular young man, the more he tugs at my heart. One thing you'll notice about his story, though: he hasn't had a dream. Yet. Let me explain.

OUTSTRIPPED IN GAZA

"I decided I wanted to go a different way."

Twenty-five-year-old Ali had spent his teen years preparing to join Hamas, but as he and I chatted over coffee in the lobby of the hotel where he works, he explained what had changed his thinking. The Grand Palace Hotel in which we sat was part of his story. The hotel offers a stunning Mediterranean view, some of the finest food in Gaza, and the best hummus anywhere in the Middle East. Fortunately for its owners, it bears no scars of the firefight in 2009 that left the mosque next door riddled with bullet holes.

In the three years before Israel's Operation Cast Lead descended upon Gaza City, some ten thousand rockets had been launched into Israel from the Strip. At some point during the storm of missiles, Hamas threw one too many at its neighbor, and the IDF took its turn at the fight. Operation Cast Lead became the moniker for Israel's retaliation due to the timing of the attack: the week of Hanukkah.

During Hanukkah, Jewish children play a game commemorating the lamp that miraculously stayed lit well after the oil had run out while the Maccabees drove Seleucid general Antiochus Epiphanes out from the temple. The pagan leader had desecrated Jerusalem by entering the Holy of Holies and sacrificing a pig on the altar. Metal dreidels used in the children's game to tell the story are traditionally cast in lead.

But during Hanukah 2009, the Israeli Defense Force was not playing games. It had one goal: to destroy Hamas.

"What made me rethink my direction in life was the war with Israel." Ali sipped coffee. I was on my second plate of hummus as he continued his story. "Hamas boasts about its strength and that it is the great defender of the Palestinians. But when Israel rolled in, I saw their real motivation.

"To avoid unnecessary casualties, Israel Defense Forces took precautions when they prepared to bomb a building. They sent text messages to civilian Palestinians warning them, 'Please get out immediately for your own safety. We are not here to hurt you. We are only after Hamas.'

"But Hamas took advantage of the Israelis' care. They actually trapped people inside so 'bystanders' would be killed. They knew reports of the battle would make Israel look bad if civilians died, so our Hamas 'protector' turned their guns on innocent people and threatened to kill them if they tried to get out. An increased body count would help the Hamas public image.

"When I heard firsthand accounts of the brutally self-serving methods Hamas used against Israel—and us!—I could hardly believe it. All my life I had heard horror stories about 'Israel, the little Satan.' But the truth was 180 degrees different. Their soldiers were trying to *protect* Palestinians while Hamas wanted us dead. The Israelis outdid our people in being humane." Ali shook his head as if he still could not quite grasp the immensity of the revelation.

"Not only did Hamas leaders try to get people killed during the battle, most of them were cowering in basements and bunkers instead of fighting. It disgusted me." Ali leaned toward me and lowered his voice. "You realize, don't you, that even now, I can tell no one how I think?"

As if on cue, drumbeats from the street disrupted conversations in the hotel lobby. We glanced through the glass front wall and watched two hundred young Hamas recruits jog by, shouting, "Death to Zionists!"

"That could have been me." Ali waved his arm at the robots streaming past the window. "Every one of those guys will probably die for the cause. There is no cause! What a waste!"

My companion leaned back into the couch and closed his eyes, as if the thought had dissipated every speck of energy from his body.

DREAMING OF DREAMS

"Ali, thank you for trusting me with your story. That means a lot to me." I suspected Ali could use some real encouragement. "I'm Christian and you're a Muslim, but I sense that you and I can talk about things in a meaningful way. What we're talking about here is not just politics. It's about what's goes on inside every man, woman, and child."

Ali opened his eyes, interested in what I might say next.

"Have you heard about a rather unusual phenomenon happening with Muslims all over the Middle East?" I asked.

"Phenomenon?" Ali twisted his lips into a half smile as he said the word. "I don't think so."

"Muslims are having dreams about Jesus. It's happening a lot.

I hear about it in every country we visit. I know you feel disheartened because of Hamas and their disregard for your people, but Jesus is honoring Arabs today. He loves them and is appearing to them regularly. I know Muslims believe Jesus is a prophet and that Muhammad even respected him greatly." I watched Ali's reaction. He was taking me seriously. "Have you ever wanted to learn more about Jesus? I can tell you one or two dream stories from anywhere you want—Lebanon, Syria, Jordan, Egypt, Iraq, Iran, Afghanistan—just pick a country."

Ali's smile broadened. "Okay," he nodded. "Iran."

I told him about another guy named Ali. I knew the Ali I was talking to would understand the significance of Jesus meeting someone who had studied at Qom.

After the first story, he asked for another. Then another. A quarter of an hour and three stories later, Ali's fascination bubbled out. "I would be honored to have a dream about Jesus." He nodded again, emphatically in my direction. "I am going to pray that I have one!"

I couldn't help but chuckle at his enthusiasm. "Me too," I promised.

Now What?

I stay in touch with Ali, and as of this writing, he hasn't told me about any dreams. Would you stop and pray for him to have a vision of Jesus and to find a local believer who can explain the gospel and lead him to Christ? And if he has had a dream by the time you read this, he can probably use your prayers more than ever.

————————————————————

NINETEEN

West Bank Story

A mina stared at the building. As she crested the hill on her walk into town, the sight of it had stopped her a hundred yards short of her destination. The young Muslim woman reached into the cloth bag slung over her right shoulder, pulled out a bottle of water, sipped the lukewarm contents, and gazed for several more minutes at the structure beside the road ahead. It was as unmistakable as her friend had said it would be. This was the building she had seen in her dream two nights ago.

Amina had learned to respect her nighttime visitations and had been positive the moment she woke up that the building was real. Dreams that last several months had been the most remarkable experience of her twenty-two years. She now knew the man who appeared to her almost every night was the great prophet Isa—Jesus. But mostly, there were things she did not know. Why would Isa pay attention to an unmarried woman in an unimportant West Bank village? Was there something He intended for her to do? What about His presence made her feel so deeply loved? Could anyone tell her what the dreams meant?

Three nights ago, she had finally talked to Jesus (she supposed it would be called praying, but to a prophet?) and asked Him every question on her mind. The next night, the building appeared to her—not Jesus, just the structure itself—and she knew she must find it.

As she resumed her walk, the front door of the building opened, and a man stepped into the afternoon sun. Amina was the closest of only three people on the street, so the man noticed her immediately and realized she was walking in his direction, a discernible purpose in her steps. He watched her approach until she was close enough that he could speak to her without shouting.

"Can I help you with something?"

Amina looked at him for an instant as if she didn't understand the question. "I'm not sure. I don't know exactly why I'm here." She realized the man did not intimidate her. There was a warmth about him that encouraged her to continue with the bizarre truth about her presence in his town. She raised her right hand numbly toward the doorway he'd come from. "I saw this building in a dream."

"I see." The man crossed his arms, raised his left hand to his face, and patted his chin. "You haven't had any other dreams recently, have you?"

Amina's eyes darted from the stranger's face to the building and back to the man. "Well, yes I have."

He looked blankly at Amina. Then his eyes brightened, and he dipped his head in greeting. "My name is Jamal. I occasionally meet people who are having dreams about Jesus. That's why I asked. I had a dream about Him myself a few years ago."

Jamal leaned close to Amina and whispered, "The Jesus dreams changed everything in my life."

Jamal invited the woman inside to talk. She replayed her questions for him and explained how long she had tried to find answers. Once she had come across a Christian television station that talked about Jesus all the time, but watching it in her home was not possible. Her father had almost caught her one time, and she decided afterward that viewing such things on the family TV was too risky. She also had dared to ask a few close friends if they ever had dreams, but none had.

For nearly three hours, Jamal and Amina talked through all she had wondered about Jesus. He concluded their time together by giving her the Bible he had used to answer many of her questions, and he offered several Christian books, which she gratefully stuffed in her bag.

At home, Amina hid her treasures, reading them only when she knew others in the family would not discover her secret life. Studying the New Testament one night, she realized that the route of Jesus' travels likely had taken Him right through her village. The town, by then, already had a long history since Canaanites had founded it long before the Israelites entered the land. The real-life drama of Jesus' time on earth riveted Amina, and several weeks after meeting Jamal, her own journey brought her to take the step of faith of becoming a Jesus follower.

Jamal had been clear about what being a disciple of Jesus would require of her, but it was tougher than she had expected. Naturally gregarious, she chafed at having no one to talk to about this growing relationship with her Savior. But months later, Amina led her sister to Christ, and the chain reaction started. Soon there were five believers in Amina's ancient village.

GUESS WHO'S COMING TO DINNER?

Amina started a house church through which she and a handful of believers planned an outreach event for Muslim women. The success of their advertising stunned them. They had hung posters promoting "A Celebration for Palestinian Women" at each mosque in two nearby villages, and on the morning of the event, more than two hundred veiled Muslims showed up.

Through Jamal, Amina had found Hannah, an American believer visiting in the West Bank, who would be the day's guest speaker. Hannah and Amina explained God's love for women and the special calling He has on their lives. Although cautious with their words, the sponsoring ladies' faces radiated the love of Jesus. Many in the audience wept as they unwrapped gifts brought from America, and at the end of Hannah's last presentation, a hundred Muslims surrounded the two women. Amina was now the one answering questions.

Alone after the last guest departed, Amina and Hannah stood together in the doorway of the meeting hall. They relished several minutes of quiet in the serene light of late afternoon before Amina spoke.

"Hannah, do you remember the energetic woman in the red hijab who talked to you after your last teaching?"

"Yes, I sure do. She was so sweet. She even invited me to her house for dinner tonight."

Amina nodded. "I've had several conversations with her, and she's always full of questions. I think Jesus is doing something in her heart." Still nodding, she looked at Hannah. "That surprises me . . ." Amina's voice trailed off.

"Why, Amina? Why does her interest in Jesus surprise you?"

"Because," Amina said, grinning at the American, "her husband is a top leader in Hamas."

Hannah's jaw dropped.

Amina swallowed a laugh. "Have a nice dinner tonight, Hannah."

PART · VIII

AFGHANISTAN—THE GATES OF HELL DON'T PREVAIL

TWENTY

The Man of Peace in "Boom!" Town

Most Americans outside of the US military would not have considered 2009 a particularly good year for travel to Afghanistan. But JoAnn and I went anyway. We were helping a friend with his assignment.

For us, Afghanistan is familiar territory after a handful of visits there, but Joel Rosenberg had never been before. At the time, he was researching his excellent book, *Inside the Revolution*,[1] and I was putting the finishing touches on *Breakthrough: The Return of Hope to the Middle East*.[2] Any first-time visit to a Middle Eastern country is an eye-opening experience for Americans, but our trip with Joel and Jeremy, his assistant, was one for the record books. What happened to us along the way was life-changing enough, and on top of that, we met a man whose encounters with Jesus were some of the most remarkable I'd heard of yet. We were totally blown away—well, almost.

Poppy Lair Demand

Joel's research included interviewing tribal leaders from a part of Afghanistan best known for providing raw materials for the immense Middle Eastern drug trade. The lucrative poppy fields hidden among the hills contribute mightily to Afghanistan's ranking as the number one supplier of opium in the world. The country is a part of the golden triangle of production for which Burma and Myanmar are the other points. Ironically, output has been on the rise since the United States invaded in 2001.

Europe in particular is a major recipient of Afghanistan's poppy harvest. The Afghans are Europe's largest supplier of heroin. Joel's favorite question became: "With so much American military presence in the country discouraging illegal drug cultivation and sales, why is the opium trade out of control?"

Tribal leaders offered assorted versions of the same answer: President Hamid Karzai and his brother, Ahmed, make it happen. Joel often mentioned a *New York Times* article published October 4, 2008, claiming that Ahmed Wali Karzai was "a major player" in the illegal trade. Any time he brought that up, the men smiled. Ahmed Karzai was not just a major player. He was *the king and master* of the billion-dollar drug trade in Afghanistan.

Convoluted relationships between the Karzai government, tribal leaders, and the Taliban, variously aligned with and against the American and European militaries, create a volcanic potential for violence that erupts regularly in the countryside and city alike.

LIFE IN THE BLAST LANE

Somewhere in Kabul the night before my wife JoAnn and Betsie, a longtime missionary in Afghanistan, headed across town in our rented van, a terrorist was busy assembling a car bomb. All too frequent in the capital city, bombs are detonated in morning or evening rush-hour traffic, timed to maximize the number of casualties. The Taliban deliver these explosive messages to remind the American military that the Taliban are still a force to be reckoned with, despite the foreigners' ten years of fighting them. Locals who oppose the Taliban understand that the message is meant for them as well.

Kabul provides world-class gridlock for its commuters, and JoAnn and Betsie were mired in the worst of it. Six lines of cars and trucks jammed the four lanes marked for traffic in each direction. When Kabul traffic moves, it's similar to Cairo's traffic, with cars going in all directions and horns blaring.

JoAnn and Betsie had resigned themselves to whatever schedule the traffic set for them and settled into conversation about how they would conduct their meeting that evening once they made it back from the Taliban village on the outskirts of the city. To hear one another over the car horns, they talked in a near-shout. Both of them grimaced when an explosion annulled all other sounds.

JoAnn told me what happened next: "Our driver yelled, 'Car bomb, car bomb!' He couldn't move the van a single inch, even though the gray sedan right next to us had just exploded. The targeted vehicle had skidded into a ditch after the bomb detonated.

"We couldn't believe what we were seeing. Our driver calmly explained that people know how these bombings can go—the ones abandoning their cars feared that a multiple bombing might have been planned—but he thought we would be safer inside. Another bomb may go off and the van would give us some protection, or terrorists waiting for the explosion might start shooting anyone in the road.

"Betsie and I felt so helpless. How can people live like this?"

Joel, Betsie, JoAnn, and I found out later just how wonderfully the Lord had protected JoAnn and Betsie. When the homemade device detonated, only part of the charge exploded. If the bomb had worked properly, it would have obliterated the gray car, our van, most of the cars around them, and everyone inside.

We realized that's why the Lord had led us to pray so hard through the night before JoAnn and Betsie left. We thought it was about the Taliban in the village they were to visit, but it was actually about the Taliban in Kabul who wanted to slaughter a bunch of people on their way home from work.

We thanked our powerful God for sparing JoAnn, Betsie, and our driver Abdul. We also prayed that the man who was the Taliban target would one day meet Jesus. I gave JoAnn the biggest hug ever, and we cried as we thought about what could have happened if the bomb had worked. I knew she would be fine, though, as soon as I heard her first comment after we dried our tears: "Now that that's over, do we have any chocolate around here?"

Later during the same Afghanistan visit, we met a man in Kabul whose life had been changed by a very different sort of meeting outside the city.

FORESTRY SERVICE

Mateen was a good-hearted Muslim and had never considered making a homemade explosive or doing intentional violence to his fellow man in any way. It troubled him that his country had been a major battleground for so many years, but he decided that blowing people up would just make it worse. So he did the best thing he could think of: he prayed.

Desperate to escape the chaos of Kabul, Mateen's favorite activity on his day off was to walk through the forests in the hill country north of the city. There he prayed—for himself, his friends, his family, his country, but especially for an end to the unending war. He asked Allah for this each time he ventured into the woods. The people of Afghanistan were tired of fighting and needed rest, and he considered his woodland prayers a service to the Afghan nation.

His prayers were consistent with what everyone knew of Mateen. Concern for others was the major focus of his life. A man of peace, Mateen believed that Muslims, even if attacked, should not retaliate. "An eye for an eye" was not his idea of justice. It was actually an example of how religion had caused so much pain and so many wars. Christians and Muslims had both started their share of violence.

Through the months, Mateen had gravitated more and more to one particular area for prayer. His favorite place was a transition valley where junipers blend with larger evergreens and the elevation keeps temperatures mild even in the raging summer months. He had learned the area well enough that he could safely leave the main path and guarantee himself several hours of solitude. He had also learned that it was the place he could count on to meet Jesus.

CURIOUS BUT NOT CONVINCED

Mateen's spiritual path to Jesus started in the streets of Kabul. His network of peace-loving friends occasionally brought him into contact with Christian believers. He enjoyed hearing them talk about how Jesus had come to bring peace with God and eventually would restore peace to the whole world. His curiosity about the Christian man of God deepened when he began working regularly with David.

The American worked for a non-government organization (NGO) project, teaching Afghan women to make a living by sewing inexpensive clothing. He needed a translator, and the organization hired Mateen for the job. Mateen was thankful he had learned English so well that he could both help this good-hearted American in his work and talk on a meaningful enough level that they could become friends as well as coworkers.

Within days of meeting Mateen, David discovered the Afghan's interest in spiritual matters and began using the Bible to give examples of how God cares for people. The sayings of Jesus and Paul about living in peace became Mateen's favorite subject of conversation, but as fascinated as he was with the two men in Scripture, the thought of leaving Islam to become a Christian was as far removed from his mind as the northern peaks from downtown Kabul. After all, for anyone who becomes a Jesus follower in a strict Islamic country like Afghanistan, persecution—or worse—is a given. Agreeing with Jesus' views on world peace was safe. Even Muhammad did that; he spoke of Isa with respect in the Qur'an.

So Mateen would enjoy both worlds, Islam and Christian, and most important, remain acceptable to his more traditional Muslim friends and family. It was the ideal plan. But then Mateen met Jesus.

Off to a Meeting

Mateen had told David about his walks in the forest, and his friend promised to pray that Mateen's time alone in the valley would bring him closer to God. To prepare for several vacation days, the two men had worked late the night before, but Mateen felt unexpectedly energized for this particular day off. He arose early and headed for his usual spot.

The crisp air freshened Mateen on his walk up the valley. He could feel the vitality in his soul, and when he arrived at his beloved cluster of junipers, he stopped and raised his arms to thank Allah for life. Mateen closed his eyes, but a peculiar sensation disturbed his focus before he could utter the first word of gratitude. He knew it before he opened his eyes: he was not alone.

A man in a white robe stood in the center of the rough circle formed by six juniper trees. Encountering anyone this far off the main path was likely not a good thing in these parts, but instead of fear, peace flooded Mateen's body. He instantly recognized the feeling as one described in a Bible verse David had read to him. Before the man spoke, Mateen also knew he was looking at Jesus.

At first, light from the man's robe fascinated Mateen the most.

215

It was bright but not harsh; he could just barely look at it without squinting. Then he saw the eyes, and Mateen couldn't look away. For several minutes, the two men talked as closest of friends. Mateen felt as if this Person had known him for his whole life—which, of course, He had. There seemed to be nothing hidden, and nothing needed to be. Even a good man like Mateen had done things to be ashamed of, but all of that was suddenly okay. Only the presence of Jesus mattered.

On the path home that afternoon, Mateen's feet felt as if they never touched the ground. *Did this really happen?* he asked himself nearly a dozen times, and each time, his soul assured him that it had. He told no one at home about the vision. He not only feared people would question his sanity and his commitment to Islam, but also, being a bit superstitious, he was afraid Jesus might not come back if he gave away the secret. That night, Mateen lay awake remembering each moment of the encounter. He wondered if he should mention it to David.

The next morning, Mateen headed to the forest again. He tried not to let himself hope Jesus would be there a second time. He didn't want the enchanting moments yesterday marred by disappointment today, but Mateen's new Friend didn't let him down. As he stepped within sight of the junipers, he could see that Jesus was waiting for him. Just like the day before, they talked, the robed man's words delving deep into Mateen's heart.

On their third day together in the woods, Jesus and Mateen began to discuss the subject that had first brought Mateen to the forest nearly a year ago. Jesus assured Mateen of His love and then spoke three sentences that changed the Afghan's life forever: "Mateen, you desire peace. But peace in this world will only be temporary. You cannot have peace that will last until you love the Prince of Peace."

For three months, Jesus met with Mateen every time he hiked the valley. Just as the Man from heaven had done with people in the Bible, He asked the peace-loving man from Afghanistan to follow Him. And like his newfound heroes in Scripture, Mateen said he would.

Still on the Path

The 2011 Operation World report indicates that Iran and Afghanistan have the two fastest growing number of churches per capita in the world![3] For both countries, it's a remarkable statistic.

Researchers estimate that when the shah of Iran was deposed in 1979 and the Islamic Republic of Iran was established, there were only five hundred believers in the entire country. Ayatollah Khomeini vowed to wipe out the church so Iran would have "only one religion." But his plan backfired. Now Iran's population includes well over one million believers.

The story in Afghanistan is similar. One imam used to boast, "There are forty-eight thousand mosques in Afghanistan and no churches." Even Christian observers agreed. Heather Mercer and Dayna Curry, American missionaries in Afghanistan and coauthors of *Prisoners of Hope*,[4] were abducted by the Taliban in Afghanistan and later rescued by the American military in 2001. Heather once told me that she remembers when there were only eight known believers in Afghanistan. Now Mateen is one of the country's approximately thirty thousand followers of Jesus.

Afghanistan remains an extremely dangerous place for believers and ranks consistently in the Top 10 Most Hostile Countries for Christians. In 2012, Open Doors ranked Afghanistan the second most dangerous country in the world for Christians to live in.[5] At one point, persecution was so severe that believers were leaving Afghanistan and climbing the border fence to escape into Iran. You know it's bad when Iran is the getaway destination! Yet Mateen's experiences with Jesus and study of Scripture have convinced him to remain among the people for whom he's prayed for so long.

"The situation has improved a little in my country," he told me, "but we are still in a war. In the midst of the uncertainty I know Jesus is with me. His great promise is never to leave us. I see that many places in the New Testament. Now I am married and have two children, and my wife loves Jesus too.

"I read the Bible every day, and Jesus is leading me to Afghans who need Him. I will serve Him for life. Even if I am persecuted, I will not stop bringing Jesus to my people."

Mateen's commitment to endure persecution is not an empty one. Although his humble spirit keeps him from sharing details of all he's been through, I know he is targeted by Islamic officials and has suffered tremendously. He's often questioned, jailed, beaten, and threatened with death by anti-Christian authorities. He counts every day as a gift because he's not sure how long he will be tolerated.

One of our conversations concluded with these sobering words from Mateen: "I am told that because I love Jesus so openly, one day I will die for my faith in Him. I know this is probably going to be what happens to me. But I am not afraid and I have the peace of God. Once He gave that to me, I had everything. Jesus is all I need. In Psalm 73:26, King David said God was his portion. That means *He alone* is enough to sustain me. The words of Jesus in John 14:15 give me strength: 'If you love me, keep my commands.'"

TWENTY-ONE

"Why Are You in Our Country?"

D oing time in an Afghanistan jail robs most prisoners of
their dignity and all of them of their hope. Except Josh
Knight. He suspected he would end up there someday,
and he did.

Enduring the subhuman conditions with joy and a smile on his
face was merely the incarcerated extension of Josh's life in the outside world. Filth on every concrete surface, plates of rancid food,
and a hole in the floor for a toilet seemed to energize the unusual
American. As a missionary, he had envisioned with anticipation
enduring such things for Christ.

The potential misery of his imprisonment was also lessened
because he didn't receive the typical beatings and because he wasn't
"left to rot." And his stay was relatively short, as trips to Kabul
prisons go.

UNWANTED SIGHTING

It seemed that Josh's release came about at least in part because
the NGO he worked with had garnered some favor with Hamid

Karzai's government. He returned to work and considered himself fairly safe living in a village an hour's drive from the capital city. That perception was shaken the moment he noticed Halik, a handsome young Afghan man, staring at him.

"Oh, not again," Josh murmured to himself. He turned his back to the man ogling him from across the marketplace. *Why is homosexuality so rampant in Afghanistan? And why is it that Americans are so often a target?*

During his handful of years in the country, Josh had received a revolting number of "offers"—most from married Afghan men who seemed fascinated with his blond hair and blue eyes. Sunny, his wife, enjoyed teasing him about his magnetism.

Those smiles make me sick to my stomach. I'm done with this market. That guy is creeping me out.

The man watching Josh wore a typical Afghan-style Payraan Tumbaan, and in the long, tan shirt, he looked like a village tribal chief. He watched his target turn away and then stepped into the crowd after Josh.

Halik's first words as he sidled up to the American missionary made an unintended impression on the Christian. "Excuse me, sir, but I need to be alone with you."

"What?" Josh wheeled in the direction of the voice he knew—and feared—was speaking to him.

"I mean, I need to visit with you right now. Will you come to my home with me?"

Josh hesitated as he decided how to answer. This was more blatant than usual. "I'm not sure that's a good idea."

The man glanced at the ground, aware that his approach was awkward for this person he so wanted to meet. "It is very important." He looked at Josh, hoping his eyes would convey the innocence of his intentions. "My name is Halik. I believe you have something to tell me. I know that God sent you."

"God?" Josh had not expected to hear that word from this man. "*God* sent me?"

"Yes! Please; I will tell you about it at my home. My wife and children will be there, too, and they also want to meet you."

Whether the statement was sincere or a smokescreen for darker purposes Josh wasn't completely sure, but he was beginning to trust the man who called himself Halik. He said a quick prayer for discernment about the nature of this particular offer and decided to pay the Afghan family a visit.

Halik surprised Josh by hailing a taxi. He had thought they would be walking. A 1980-something Fiat, sporting three different colored side panels—the markings of a vehicle with a rich history of accidents—scooped up Halik and his guest and honked its way out of the market toward the Afghan's residence. Ten minutes later, they stepped onto a dust-covered apartment floor that served as a conference table for Josh's meeting with Halik, his wife, and three young children.

EXTENDED CONVERSATION

Halik's wife Leena served tea. Then Halik opened the discussion.

"Why are you in our country?"

Surprised again, the question worried Josh in yet another way. Could this man be a spy for the local imams? He had practiced his religiously neutral, humanitarian aid monologue many times, so his response flowed naturally. "I'm just trying to help people in a time of war. I know it is hard to live here, and I hope to bring some light to a dark situation."

Halik's eyes didn't budge from Josh's. "No. What are you really doing here?"

Startled at the intensity of Halik's retort, Josh blurted a question back: "Why does it matter to you what I'm doing here?"

Halik's face softened. "Because you have been in my dreams for the last seven nights in a row. When I saw you come into the market, that's why I could not take my eyes off you. A man named Jesus told me last night that you have a message for me. He told me that my wife and children should hear what you have to say as well." Now his eyes and words pleaded together, "Sir! What is this message you have from Jesus?"

Josh's afternoon tea with Halik's family grew into a three-day retreat. Just before dinner on the first day, Josh texted Sunny to assure her that he had not been kidnapped by the Taliban. His brief account of the day thrilled the fellow missionary, and she promised to pray for him as long as he needed to be away. The man of the house had evidently described every dream to his wife and children. They all wondered what the visits could mean.

That Halik could not read well enough to understand the Qur'an on his own simplified Josh's task of providing answers. Halik's knowledge of Islam was derived only from the little he had learned from their imam. Most of his belief system consisted of superstitious mush.

Leena's intensity matched her husband's. Once when Josh asked if she had questions of her own, she chattered for an hour, detailing her reflections on Halik's experiences. Her insights impressed

Josh. After a second hour of thoughts and questions from Leena, Josh noticed that all three children still sat silently, drinking in each word. He knew these people were on their way to becoming a family in love with Jesus.

THE DAYS AFTER

Halik and Leena accepted Christ into their lives, and with Josh and Sunny as mentors, grew quickly into their community's strongest believers. They now lead a house church and as many as twenty people cram into their apartment for late-night services.

Halik now understands what the people of his country need most. He said, "The message of Jesus is what will bring the freedom that Afghans have wanted for decades. This is our hope. We have searched for it through religion, politics, and war. But those are dead-end streets, and none of them will ever bring freedom. I am a free man. And Jesus did this for me."

PART · IX

AMERICA—LOVING
MUSLIMS TO CHRIST

TWENTY-TWO

A Veiled Threat

As I bring the stories in this book closer to home, I hope
you'll bear with me if I preach a little bit. Many of you
will have the chance to see the very opportunities God
brought to the folks I tell about here right in your own neighbor-
hoods. To take advantage of the potential, though, you may have
a few things to learn, and a touch of preaching might help you
get there.

JUST START IT!

In chapter 7, you'll recall, I introduced you to Hormoz Shariat,
the host of the television talk show Iran Alive! whom Dina used
to call from Iran. I know some of his stories because he's told me
about them. Others I know because I took part in them. This is
one of those.

Several years ago, Hormoz and I felt we should do something
to share with believers in America as much as we could about

what we'd learned about Muslims. Most believers here have no contact with Muslims. Even if they're right in the same neighborhood, many American churchgoers don't know where to begin in establishing a relationship. Others simply don't want to.

So we developed a fast-paced, fact-filled, church-based seminar packed with helpful background information and practical ideas for reaching out to Muslims. We show videos, hear testimonies of former Muslims, and explain creative ways to get believers engaged through prayer, acts of service, and outreach.

We knew we were onto something. As we listened to comments and questions that came up over and over among participants, here is some of what we heard:

- "I have Muslim neighbors, and I have never even attempted to meet them. I am convicted and ashamed of myself."
- "I thought all Muslims were terrorists and needed to be deported."
- "I have been expecting our government to deal with Muslims and protect us. Never once did I think about sharing Jesus with them."
- "Why is it that Muslims never speak out against terrorism? Why do they keep silent? Are they afraid of retaliation from fundamentalist Muslims?"

As in most large groups, you find a variety of beliefs and preconceived ideas. Our goal is to reorient people's thinking, alleviate their fears, and mobilize them to action. Most of the churches in which Hormoz and I teach are Bible-believing congregations that preach the Word, disciple new believers, worship passionately, and want to reach their communities with the gospel. With a few tools, they are making a difference. One of them is Horizon Christian Fellowship, pastored by Mike MacIntosh. Mike has a heart for God and he is a pastor's pastor. He and I became friends after Joel Rosenberg suggested we film our seminar at his church.

"There are Muslims in our neighborhood, and I have no relationship with them," Mike admitted to me. "I haven't even tried. But I know God wants me to reach out to them. What do I do to get started?"

I love the "how to get started" question.

"At one time, I was where you are," I told Mike. "I avoided Muslims and didn't want anything to do with them. But God changed my heart. Your comment tells me that you're open to changing, too, so here's what you can do. Start with the mosque across the street from the church, and prayer walk around it once a week. After that, why don't you meet the imam?"

"I never thought about meeting the imam. How do I do that?"

"Just go meet him and invite him to coffee. Ask him if there is anything you can do for him. Mike, just treat him like Jesus would."

"Will he try to convert me to Islam?"

"C'mon, Mr. Evangelist. Of course he will. Wouldn't you expect him to try?"

"Yeah, I guess so."

"Think of it this way, Mike. Once he tells *you* about Muhammad, then you get to tell *him* about Jesus."

A Seminar Passes the Test

Mike's sensitivity to the needs of Muslims made his church a prime spot to hold one of our seminars. The seminar we hosted at his church helped launch their ministry efforts, but not quite the way we expected.

If things hadn't turned out so incredibly well, we might have had a real fiasco on our hands, because the church advertised the seminar in the newspaper. Normally, Hormoz and I discourage anyone from blaring something about "How to Love Muslims to Christ" in the local paper. It can prompt a showdown with Muslims instead of an opportunity. But a couple of weeks before the event, the church's ad appeared.

The ad generated some pushback, but it was well worth it. On Tuesday night, a Muslim woman wearing a hijab showed up for the Wednesday seminar. She was a day early. Tuesday, though, is ladies Bible study night. Seeing a woman wandering around the campus, the Bible study leader walked up to Nasreen and asked if she needed help.

From behind her veil, the young woman explained. "Yes, I read in the newspaper that you're having a seminar on 'How Christians Should Love Muslims.' I wanted to see what that was about. Where are you having this discussion?"

Nasreen had read the title wrong but was drawn to the church to see how she could get in on some of this *loving Muslims* stuff. She had not lived in America long and was feeling lonely. She wanted a friend.

Nasreen had run into many people who were repelled by her traditional garb, especially the veil, but not Sandy. Sandy prayed a quick prayer and answered Nasreen, "Well, the seminar is tomorrow night, but we have a women's Bible study this evening. Will you join us? Our study is on the topic of love. I think you'd enjoy it, and we would be honored to have you come!"

Nasreen jumped at the invitation, and as Sandy led her into the fellowship hall, the women's leader prayed that none of the ladies would fall out of their chairs at seeing a veiled Muslim woman walk in.

But the women overwhelmed Nasreen with love, and their Muslim guest responded by revealing that she had been wanting to know more about Jesus for quite some time. The group might have been less shocked about *why*, though, if they had known more about how God is working among Middle Easterners these days.

"He's already told me that He loves me." Nasreen summarized her dreams about Jesus as matter of factly as if she were explaining that she had eaten dinner that evening. He had visited her most nights during the past few weeks, and she had many questions the Bible discussion had begun to answer.

At the end of the study, every woman in the group hugged Nasreen. She could hardly believe the genuine warmth of these people, and the next night, Nasreen was in the congregation when our seminar began.

Hormoz and I will never forget that evening at Horizon Christian Fellowship. Hearts were so tuned to the need for ministry to Muslims that when our video of Iranian believers worshipping in an underground church came on the screen, most of the assembly dissolved in tears. The experience touched Nasreen, and she committed that night to become a follower of the Man in her dreams.

Next Steps

What about you? Jesus wants your heart for reaching people who need Him. He may need to perform surgery and clear out your arteries, but you can trust Him to do it the best way for you. If your arteries are like mine were, there's a lot of junk in there, and He wants to get rid of the stuff that has no business in a follower of Christ. Fear, anger, complacency, and judgmentalism need to go.

Letting Jesus clean out the mess worked for me (or I wouldn't be writing this book). And it worked for Sandy. If she had not let Jesus prepare her heart, Nasreen would have walked that church campus a few minutes longer and then gone home—probably for good.

So, thank you Horizon Christian Fellowship, pastor Mike, Sandy, and all churches opening their arms to Muslims. You overcame your fears of reaching out, and I am sure God will give you many more opportunities to lead these people to His Son.

TWENTY-THREE

Muslim Boy in Bible Town

On September 25, 2009, the Jummah Prayer Gathering met on Capitol Hill in Washington, DC, for "A Day of Islamic Unity." Organizers planned for fifty thousand Muslims on the Capitol steps praying to Allah and reading from the Qur'an.

As soon as the event's press releases hit the news, a wave of negative publicity gushed into the media, and Christian groups were some of the most vocal opponents of the rally. Detractors viewed the Islamic prayer event as a threat to our country. Because Muslim extremists had attacked the nation just eight years earlier, many Americans had a hard time comprehending that the organizers were anything but a gang of Islamic terrorists. The controversial "Ground Zero Mosque" also factored into the tempest of animosity. Former Muslims in the Middle East often questioned me about the proposed mosque at the site of the 911 attack. They saw it as a Muslim "statement of victory" over America. So did I.

So, to many Americans, the idea that Muslims could worship Allah at the US Capitol was just going too far. I understand the thinking. My father was an FBI agent, and we Doyles want the US to be secure from any kind of terrorist threats.

I heard a rash of bitter complaints like this:

- "Not on our Capitol steps!"
- "Let's protest this injustice!"
- "If they want to pray to Allah, let them go back to the Middle East and do it there."

I had to ask myself, "What if they were well-meaning people who just wanted to pray?" The answer was obvious: we should let them pray because America is a free country. We've been blessed to have Christian groups pray on the Capitol steps. We've had Jews pray on the Capitol steps. If the Muslims doing it were not a threat to national security, then they ought to be allowed to pray there too.

SHOWDOWN AT THE CAPITOL

Muslim faithful began arriving at dawn on September 25 for the fifteen-hour prayer vigil. Protestors greeted them with graphic signs denigrating the people assembling to pray. Angry demonstrators—many of them representing Christian organizations that had publicly opposed the event—lined the side of Constitution Avenue designated as their territory and screamed vindictive slogans at the calmer crowds across the street. The message was unmistakable: Muslims are not welcome in America.

On the more sedate side of the street, a contingent of believers ministered to the Muslims throughout the day, serving them sandwiches and water. Some even played with their children. While they did not condone all that went on in the Muslim gathering, they tried to make a loving impact for Christ.

The image of the opposing crowds left me with a significant question every believer needs to answer: which side of the street do you want to be on?

Do we really think protest signs are the way to share Christ? Even if some of the objections about Islam spelled out on posters that day were true, the anger and even hatred was hardly a magnet that would draw people to Jesus.

Years ago, I participated in a Right to Life march in Texas with JoAnn and some of our children. As the opposition spit on us and cursed in our faces, I remember thinking, *Wow, I could lose it here and really punch someone!* So if I were Muslim at the DC prayer rally? I probably would have felt the same way.

To offer love to the followers of Islam is not unpatriotic. I'm an American and want our nation to be safe just as much as anyone. I'm proud of what we are; my father served in the US Air Force in World War II and worked for thirty years as an FBI agent. But remember this: *not all Muslims are terrorists.* We need to remind ourselves of that occasionally to offset what we see on the news.

It also helps to keep in mind that many Muslims who have immigrated to America are *cultural Muslims only.* They were born Muslim but have never practiced their religion. Some have even come here to escape the radical Muslim cultures of the Middle East. But whether Muslims practice their religion or not, both groups need Jesus. As believers, the best thing we can do is to show them who Jesus is. Half a country away from the US Capitol, that's how Mirna and her son were introduced to the Savior—that and a dream or two.

WHEATON RIPE FOR HARVEST

With her husband and son, Mirna fled the war in Iraq and settled in metropolitan Chicago. At the time the three found their new family home, they didn't realize the spiritual implications of living in Wheaton, Illinois.

The Chicago suburb is a rich habitat for evangelical Christians. Within a radius of just a few miles, influential Christian ministries abound, such as *Christianity Today*, Wheaton Bible College, Good News/Crossway Publishers, Tyndale House Publishers, and Wheaton Bible Church. This town, where countless residents name their children after Billy Graham and Jim Elliott, was an awkward place for a fifteen-year-old Muslim boy named Mohammad.

Yet, as Mohammad eventually discovered, he was not the only one of his kind in the area. He and the growing cluster of other Muslims attracted the attention of pastor Rob Bugh and his mission team at Wheaton Bible Church. Convinced that their congregation should do something to reach these neighbors, WBC did the best thing they could think of: the church started a Sunday school class for Muslims.

It also turned out to be the best thing ever for Mirna and her boy.

After several meetings at the church, Mohammad's mother was so touched by the love of Christians for her Muslim family that she wanted to know more about Jesus and His followers. So she asked God for a sign—and got one.

The week after she made her request of whatever divine being she assumed was listening, Mohammad began having dreams about Jesus. He was nonchalant the morning after the first dream, not quite believing his nighttime meeting with the prophet was real. What were dreams anyway? But his mother knew her prayer had been answered. The next night, Mohammad had a harder time ignoring his encounter, and by the third time Jesus appeared, he woke his mother up long before dawn to tell her the details.

For reasons still not clear, the dreams have come only to Mohammad, yet Mirna is the one who's been deeply changed by the experience. Mohammad's dreams supplemented the teaching at church and quickly convinced her that Jesus is indeed the Son of God and the Savior that she needed.

Shortly before I wrote this chapter, Mirna accepted Christ. And as for Mohammad? He's getting closer every day. You might want to say a prayer for him right now.

Extreme Discipleship

B eing a genuine disciple of Jesus has never been easy. For all of us, growth takes time and obstacles always seem to roll into the path. But the difficulty of the process and the cost for Muslims may never have been greater than it is today. They face hardships that rival any the persecuted church has endured through the centuries. That's why dreams alone aren't enough. No one goes to sleep a Muslim and wakes up a Christian. Jesus' personal appearances are an incredible work, but He still uses godly people to share the gospel that brings salvation.

Dreams and visions break down barriers that keep Muslims from embracing Christ. Then it's up to us to get the gospel to them with a solid explanation and an offer to receive Jesus.

How Legit Is Their Faith?

As I share stories in American churches about Rashid from Jordan, Mateen from Afghanistan, Dina from Iran, and others, I am often asked, "How do you know that these people truly became believers?"

My answer is simple: "Because they are willing to die for Jesus." That's a good litmus test, don't you think?

Jesus never backed away from this prerequisite for discipleship. In Matthew 10:38–39, He explained, "Whoever does not take up their cross and follow me is not worthy of me. Whoever finds their life will lose it, and whoever loses their life for my sake will find it."

I encourage you not to take lightly the sacrifice required of Muslims who want to come to Christ. How would people in your church respond if the bottom-line, dead-serious question asked of everyone in your Newcomers Class was: "Are you willing to die for Jesus?" Can you imagine wrapping up with your new members this way: "Before you become a member of our church, we just have one last question: are you willing to die for Jesus if you are called on to do so?"

Many would probably answer: "Hm. I think I'll try the other church down the street!" And yet that is exactly what virtually every new believer in a Muslim country is being asked.

No wonder God's compassion compels Him to make personal visits that encourage them in their walk toward Him. Better than we, Jesus recognizes the afflictions they will face. Former Muslims who have had dreams about Jesus, receive His offer of salvation, and become His disciples *are willing to die for the One who appeared to them.*

Another reason I can assure people that the faith of Muslim-background believers is real is that they often bear very much spiritual fruit. Passionate about their faith in Christ, they influence others to follow Jesus like no other group of people I have ever seen.

In John 15, Jesus lays out His desire for our lives as His followers: "This is to my Father's glory, that you bear much fruit, showing yourselves to be my disciples" (John 15:8). He wants us to bear fruit.

Former Muslims who become followers of Christ also cling to Him urgently. Many times, like Amina in the West Bank, a Muslim-background believer is the only follower of Jesus in his or her village. As Muslim converts persevere, though, their influence inevitably spreads—bears fruit—often far beyond their hometowns.

Henry Dineen, a good friend and president of the dynamic ministry Greater Europe Missions, once voiced a concern to me about the status of the church in Europe because it is far from the powerhouse it used to be. At one time, the gospel had a major impact on European culture and robust churches from England, Scotland, and other countries launched the modern missions movement. Not so much anymore.

Henry said, "I wonder what it is going to take to wake up the European church."

Fresh from a trip to the Middle East, I suggested a strategy you might call reverse engineering: "I think we should concentrate our efforts on reaching the Muslims in Europe and then let them reach the European church."

The power behind the idea is that, when Muslims embrace Jesus Christ, they usually have a fire for God that is rarely seen in our "less emotional" Western cultures, and their passion is contagious. Muslims who have dreams and visions about Jesus and end up becoming His followers lead others to Christ, are passionate for

Jesus, and are willing to die for their faith. Their faith sounds legit to me.

What's That Ticking?

Another observation I've made in talking to American believers about reaching out to Muslims is that the first emotion they often experience is fear. For most of my life, I must confess, I felt the same way when thinking of the people of Islam. But Jesus shook me up and basically told me to "get a grip." Is the gospel for all people everywhere or just the ones we feel comfortable with?

Americans watch way too much news provided by major networks that are part of the entertainment industry. That means these newscasts are heavily motivated by ratings. And one sure way to get an audience is to lead with a story that has the word *terrorism*. The image of Muslims blowing up everyone who gets in their way sticks in our minds, and soon we are paralyzed with fear.

When I speak in churches, I often ask, "What's the first thing you think of when you hear the word *Palestinian* (or *Syrian* or *Iranian* or *Arab*)?"

The answer is always the same: "Terrorist!" Sometimes the response is so loud and unanimous I've found myself thinking that the pastor would probably give anything to hear such a heartfelt "Amen!" during a sermon.

Some Muslims, of course, are terrorists—a significant number, in fact. Many Islamists take a literal view of the Qur'an that leads them right into jihad. Worldwide, roughly 10 percent of Muslims fall into this category. So if Islam claims 1.5 billion total followers, then 150 million of them are hard-liners who believe terrorism is acceptable and that jihad is the way to be a good Muslim.

But what about the other 90 percent? Most Muslims I meet are warm and friendly. If you do not know a Muslim personally or have never been to the Middle East, you may be surprised to hear that.

When I reflect on Muslims in the Middle East, I don't think of bombs ticking. The "ticking" I hear is a clock. It's getting late, and we're in an urgent period of time. Throughout the twenty-century history of Jesus' church, God has focused on different people groups in various eras. There have been great awakenings in Asia, South America, Europe, the United States, and Africa. Today, God is reaching out to multiple people groups that have one thing in common: a huge proportion of the people are Muslim. And many of them are finding out about Jesus through dreams and visions. He is reaching out to people in a religion spread all over the globe.

How long will this last? I don't know. Patterns of the past suggest that Muslims will continue to have dreams and visions for a while, but then it will end. After that, God may concentrate on Hindus or Buddhists, or maybe even atheists. On the other hand, the return of Jesus may be next. So what does this ticking clock mean to you and me?

GOD'S MOVING AMONG MUSLIMS SHOULD MOVE YOU

I mentioned earlier an advertisement about dreams that appeared in a newspaper in Cairo. Here's one from a 2011 newspaper in

Ramallah, West Bank: "The man in a white robe that you met in your dream has a message for you. Call this number . . ."

These ads underscore that God is moving. And His movement is not just a wiggle here and there. It's more like a massive earthquake in the Muslim world. As the Muslim proportion of the global population nears 25 percent, you can either view that as a threat to international stability or as an opportunity for the body of Christ. I believe God's actions in the Middle East over the last two decades make it clear which view God takes. These fields have never been riper for the harvest.

During Jesus' ministry on earth, He chose followers from backgrounds that raised a lot of traditional eyebrows: a harlot, a tax collector, an insurrectionist, a foul-mouthed fisherman, a skeptic. Their profile shot to smithereens the theory "I'm not good enough to become one of His disciples." The bias of many Christians I know would throw "Muslim" in with that nontraditional group, but what does Jesus do with people like that? He moves in their direction. As His followers, we need to get in line and follow the Master—if we're up to the task.

WHERE HAVE ALL THE DISCIPLES GONE?

Surveys show that 51 percent of Americans claim to be Christian. But if we are the majority, why aren't we making a massive impact on our country? Why is the United States regarded around the world as such an immoral country? Although we ought to be turning back evil and gaining ground morally, church attendance has remained level for about twenty years—hence, our cultural slide into depravity.

If you wonder how this can be, I believe I have an answer. The problem is in the way we talk about ourselves. Jesus never called us to be "Christians." He called people to be His disciples. And there is a big difference between the two.

Depending on which translation of the New Testament you read, the word *Christian* is used 10 times or fewer. The word *disciple*, however, shows up about 260 times. *Disciple* means a "learner and a follower" and carries with it an ongoing, present-tense emphasis. A disciple is someone whose faith is lived out each day. People who understand the Middle East grasp the distinction.

Ronnie, a Jewish believer I met in Israel, once said to me, "Tom, do me a favor and don't use the word *Christian* when you're over here."

This idea was new to me at the time, so I asked him why.

"Because in the Middle East, it doesn't mean what you intend it to mean. In Lebanon, it's a political party. And remember the Crusades? *Christian* conjures up some bad stereotypes. Please use the terms *believer* or *follower of Christ*. Or better yet, use the word *disciple*."

To be the type of disciple Ronnie is talking about, you don't have to relocate to the Middle East. If you open your eyes to God's moving, you'll find the chance right where you live.

IF A MUSLIM MOVES IN NEXT DOOR, DON'T CALL 911

As uneasy as it might make you feel, a Muslim moving in next door does not constitute a reason to call the police department. But it does constitute a reason to "radicalize" your own following of Jesus. Islam is spreading in America as Muslims immigrate here (most often legally). The fact that they have come to America indicates something is missing in their lives. They may need a better job, a college education, or perhaps they are simply looking for a better life. Whatever the reason, they are coming.

At some point, it is likely that a Muslim family will move into your neighborhood. If so, you'll have a choice to make. Are you going to ignore them and hope they go away? Pack up and move somewhere else yourself? Or open your arms and welcome them to town?

I can tell you that Jesus won't ignore them, and He won't flee the neighborhood. So you might as well hang out where He is— right with your Muslim neighbors. Show them Jesus' love. Invite them over for dinner. Welcome them to the neighborhood. Get to know them. Who knows? You might hear some great dream stories!

I'll caution you about one thing, though. If Jesus fills your heart with love for Muslims, you put away your fear. And as you develop friendships with them, some people—even in your church—will say you've gone overboard, that you're too extreme. And if so, welcome to the club. I get that tag put on me all the time. And what a compliment it is. According to the New Testament, a disciple like that will follow Jesus anywhere (even next door). We live in extreme times, and extreme times demand extreme disciples.

THE NON-SEEKER CHURCH

This book opened with the verse Isaiah 65:1: "I revealed myself to those who did not ask for me; I was found by those who did not seek me."

The great Jewish prophet Isaiah wrote those words twenty-seven hundred years ago as a warning to Israel that God would open the doors of His kingdom to people other than the Jews if Israel turned from Him. We know now that it was a foreshadowing of God's long-term plan to bring Gentiles into His family. Paul makes this clear in Romans 10, the passage in which he agonizes over his people—the Jews—and their rejection of Jesus the Messiah. He proclaims that the benefits of the death, burial, and resurrection of Jesus Christ now extend to Gentiles: "For there is no difference between Jew and Gentile." And he declares, "Everyone who calls on the name of the Lord will be saved" (Romans 10:12–13).

In the first-century church, the question of Gentiles being included within the body of Christ sparked a great debate that triggered the Jerusalem Council described in Acts 15. James summarized the intent of the gospel when he addressed the assembly with these words in verse 19: "It is my judgment, therefore, that we should not make it difficult for the Gentiles who are turning to God."

As I hope this book has demonstrated, Paul's application of Isaiah's and James's proclamation to the council applies to Muslims becoming followers of Jesus today. God Himself is reaching out to Muslims in a new and miraculous way, and they are being saved in record numbers. In the spirit of the apostles, then, we who ourselves are grafted into God's family should welcome Muslim-background believers with open arms.

As we close, I leave you with a prayer I hope you will offer regularly for our Muslim brothers- and sisters-to-be:

Lord, we thank You for Your great love and tender mercies.
How awesome You are. We worship You in spirit and truth.

In Your amazing grace, You love all of us equally and intimately, regardless of the color of our skin, our gender, the language we speak, or the country in which we live. You, Lord, desire that each of us, as Your unique creation, will come to know You in a saving relationship.

You have paid the ultimate price in sacrificing Your only Son, Jesus, to restore fellowship with us that was broken through our sins, and You continue to reach us with unrestrained boundaries today. You use Your amazing Word to transform lives.

May each man and woman who picks up this book be overwhelmed by You. We ask You to break their hearts for the 1.5 billion Muslims who desperately need Jesus. We ask You to call followers of Jesus everywhere to action.

Thank You for opening the hearts and minds of Muslims through dreams and visions that set them on a path to Jesus. We pray that Your Spirit and presence will continue to draw people in the Islamic world to You. And give strength to those who respond to your call.

In the name of Jesus, amen.

A Brief History of
Visits from Jesus

The current drama is not the first time Jesus has arrived in force to reel people in from the devil. To fully appreciate today's drama with God, I'd like to share for a moment how it fits with other offensives He's launched before.

Throughout the history of Jesus' church, there have been times when His obvious presence was seen and felt intensely. These supernatural breakthroughs don't occur every decade or even every century, but when they do, God's fingerprints are unmistakable, and the spiritual landscape changes radically. Here's a rundown on some of the most significant periods the church has experienced.

The Apostolic Age of the first century was the initial breakthrough because it set the pattern for the expansion of the gospel and the price that followers of Christ would have to pay to accomplish the Great Commission. Jesus gave the apostles and other New Testament heroes strength to face the onslaught of persecution that actually propelled the church into "all the world."

The Church Council Age from 325 to 787 appears on the surface to be anything but a supernatural breakthrough period. Conflict, controversy, intrachurch fighting and continuous charges of heresy became synonymous with this divisive period. But the seven major church councils spurred by the struggle helped define core beliefs and set theological parameters within which the church still operates today. Despite this period of civil war within the church, God guided His faithful ones through the upheaval and produced a powerful church.

The Reformation Age from 1521 to 1610 centered the church on *sola fide*—faith alone for salvation—as Martin Luther led the break from the Roman Church. Luther's insistence on faith in Christ's atonement to save, rather than a person's own works, brought division once again. He, along with others like Zwingli and Calvin, launched the Protestant movement and forced Christians to recognize a personal salvation experience rather than one supposedly dispensed by church leaders. This truth still guides the church today.

The Great Awakening of the 1700s built the foundation of the church in the United States. God moved through men like Jonathan Edwards, George Whitfield, and the Wesley brothers to bring the body of Christ to repentance while America was in its colonial period. Since then the US has launched more mission organizations, sent more missionaries, and financed more missionary works than any other nation in history. And preachers like D. L. Moody and Billy Graham were driven by the power that emanated from the Great Awakening.

The Missionary Movement in eighteenth- and nineteenth-century England found God using men like William Carey to mobilize the church. Zealous pioneers risked their lives to spread the gospel. Carey's motto, "Expect great things from God; attempt great things for God," became the heart cry of missionaries for generations that followed.

We can review each divine breakthrough and see vividly the full impact of God's presence. Years from now—whether before or after the Lord's return—we will no doubt look back at our time and see a stunning picture of all that God has done in the current wondrous breakthrough. I believe we're seeing the Great Awakening of the Muslim world. What God is accomplishing in our world today is even more magnificent when you consider what the adversary has done through the centuries to solidify his hold on Muslims.

Real or Fake? A Biblical Test for Dreams and Visions

D reams and visions are a part of our Judeo-Christian foundation. The major difference between supernatural biblical experiences and today's dreams is clear: the dreams of Scripture gave *revelation* to leaders of Israel, the church, and even to pagan kings, but the dreams Muslims are receiving today give *insight* into the person of Jesus and His offer of salvation. To affirm the validity of dreams as a way to hear from God, I've outlined below a number of dream and vision events detailed in Scripture.

JACOB'S LADDER DREAM

In Genesis 28, God gave Jacob a dream in an important place: the land God said Isaac and his descendants would inherit. Jacob's dream confirmed an earlier promise God had made in Genesis 25, that Jacob's older brother would serve the younger brother. It was timely because, after Jacob had schemed and stolen Esau's birthright, he doubted that God would support this unusual arrangement. The dream is pivotal to the Jewish race and to the identification of the Messiah.

PHARAOH'S FAMINE DREAM

Wise men and magicians of Egypt received their power from Satan, and over the centuries, they manipulated Pharaoh and the people into idolatry and all-out paganism. But Pharaoh's dreams in Genesis 41 came from the God of Israel, and the usual dream team was powerless to interpret it. When Joseph explained the detailed dreams and warned the king to prepare for a massive famine, Joseph became the number two man in Egypt. From his position, Joseph saved his own family line—and the Hebrew people.

DANIEL'S END-TIMES VISIONS

While living in Babylon, Daniel dreamed dreams and also interpreted them. But when it came to interpreting the king's dream in Daniel 8, he faced the ultimate challenge: recount the king's dream without first being told; then explain what it means.

In this double-dream scenario, the night before Daniel is to appear before the king, God reveals the king's dream and its interpretation to Daniel. The dream detailed a blueprint of world leadership for the next several centuries.

Later, in chapters 9 through 12, the angel Gabriel revealed to Daniel one of the greatest visions of the entire Bible. In it, the major end-times players are laid out. It explains the role of Antichrist and even speaks of a temple that will be standing in Jerusalem during the time of the tribulation.

Daniel's visions have a consistent theme and purpose: to warn of an evil ruler who will set himself up in opposition to God. Those who follow the Lord of heaven will resist that ruler and be victorious. A summary of Daniel's core message is "Be watchful, and be warned."

Gospel Dreams and Visions

Dreams and visions in the first four books of the New Testament include:

- The angel Gabriel appeared to Zechariah the priest and announced that he and his wife Elizabeth would be parents of John, the one who would prepare the way of the Lord.
- Gabriel announced the upcoming birth of Jesus to a stunned but willing unwed mother.
- Joseph received assurance from an angel that Mary was telling the truth and that he should not divorce her.
- Likely, this is the same angel who appeared to Joseph after Jesus was born to let him know King Herod wanted to kill Jesus.
- An angel appeared to Joseph a third time to tell him the coast was clear and Herod was dead so he, Mary, and Jesus could return home.

PETER'S GENTILE VISION

In Acts 10, God brought together the apostle Peter and a Roman soldier through a pair of visions. The results of their visions and their meeting are the reason we Gentiles can follow our Jewish Messiah today. At the cross, Jesus destroyed the dividing wall between Jew and Gentile, and Acts 10 is when Peter gets the picture in high definition.

God used Peter's vision to unlock the gates of the church, take down the Gentiles Not Welcome sign, and throw it in the Mediterranean Sea. The visions of Cornelius and Peter catapulted the church out of Israel and sent disciples to the ends of the earth. Even though Jesus had told them to do this in the Great Commission, the church had remained in Israel. In next chapter of Acts after the vision stories, church evangelists went on their first mission trip.

PAUL'S CONVERSION VISION

If Paul were alive today and you met him before his conversion, you would probably call him a terrorist. Today he would be fire-bombing, delivering explosive Purim packages, and trying to kill every Jewish convert he could. Why do I say this? When Stephen became the first martyr of the church, Saul (Paul's old name) was standing by, giving a standing ovation; and when Saul had his vision on the way to Damascus, he was going there to slaughter Christians.

The distance between Jerusalem and Damascus is only 135 miles. Since a "day's journey" in biblical days was about twenty miles, it was a one-week trip. That must have seemed like nothing to Saul as he neared Damascus, one of the oldest cities in the world.

His fight against the Way knew no boundaries. By obtaining official letters from the high priest in Jerusalem, Saul was free to raid every synagogue in Damascus in search of defectors. They would become his prisoners and have a one-week journey back to Jerusalem. Who could imagine what awaited them there? If Saul had his way, they would end up under a pile of rocks just outside the city gates like Stephen.

But within a few seconds, Saul went from aggressive persecutor to helpless captive. An intense light from heaven blinded him, and he hit the ground, paralyzed with fear. The Lord introduced Himself personally to Saul: "I am Jesus, whom you are persecuting" (Acts 9:5).

Paul's vision redefined the rest of his life. Ironically, he became everything that he had opposed as the main persecutor of the young church:

- Saul the Pharisee persecuted the church and tried to destroy it; Paul the Apostle received persecution and did not fight back.
- Saul the Pharisee advanced in Judaism and was zealous for tradition; Paul the Apostle advanced the gospel and wrote thirteen New Testament books.
- Saul the Pharisee brought Jews back to Jerusalem to bind them to the Law; Paul the Apostle went from Jerusalem to the Gentiles to offer free grace.
- Saul the Pharisee tried to kill believers; Paul the Apostle was killed for being a believer.

JESUS DREAMS TODAY

As I've observed the pattern of dreams and visions among Muslims today, I've recognized some characteristics common to legitimate visitations from Jesus. My five Dream Principles are noted below.

1. The dreams do not suggest anything not supported by promises contained in the Word of God. If the dream portrays Jesus in a different light than what we see in Scripture, the dream is a false one. If the plan of Jesus, His purposes, or His character is altered in a dream, then it's an open-and-shut case: this message doesn't originate from God. Instead, it is an example of what Paul warned us about: Satan disguising himself as an angel of light. Even though God uses dreams and visions, it's also true that most cults started with one, so it's crucial to measure whatever someone sees by Scripture.

2. Muslims who have dreams about Jesus remember the experience, complete with the concrete details. The specifics stay with that person. I've talked with dreamers who, even ten years after their dream experience, can recount every component of it. Dreams that have no meaning or are merely naturally occurring dreams are usually forgotten the next day. Even if they are frightening, the fear is gone shortly afterward.

3. Muslims who have dreams about Jesus realize their experience is purposeful and that it is not a stand-alone event. The dream launches them on a quest to know more. Since humans have a deep-down desire to know God, the dream

gives the spiritually thirsty a drink of water, but it doesn't quench their thirst. Only the Living Water provided by a salvation experience with Christ can do that.

4. When Muslims have dreams about Jesus, they realize a new order is in store. They grasp that Jesus loves them and welcomes them. This leads them on a search to know Jesus personally. Once they find Him in all His glory, many Muslims have no trouble repenting of their sins and committing to follow Jesus for the rest of their lives. Once they sense Jesus' love, they are drawn to Him just like Cornelius was drawn to the God of Israel.

5. A dream or a vision about Jesus brings definition to a Muslim's life. The dreamer cannot shake off the encounter. It becomes part of his or her personal testimony on the way to knowing Jesus.

The Global Shift—Christianity Soars Ahead of Islam

D avid Garrison, author of *Church Planting Movements*, offers the following encouraging statistics about the growth of Christianity:

The annual global growth rate is currently

- 2.6 percent for evangelicals
- 1.2 percent for historical Christians
- 1.2 percent for the world population growth
- 1.9 percent for Islam[1]

We also know from research that

- The majority of Islamic growth is through birth. An estimated 96 percent of Muslim growth is merely biological. Since Islamic tradition values large families, this inflates the numbers in their favor.

- The majority of evangelical growth is through conversion. The 2000 edition of the *World Christian Encyclopedia* gives these conversation rates:
  - Annually, 950,000 people become Muslims.
  - Annually, 2.7 million people become Christians.
  - For every 1 Muslim conversion, there are 3 Christian conversions.
- It is estimated that 82,000 new believers are added to the body of Christ every day. These are true converts who have repented of their sins and embraced Jesus as their Savior. Islam, on the other hand, often uses threats and persecution to build up the ranks. These "conversions" are not based on conviction but are merely survival techniques.
- 85 percent of the world has a Bible available in the native language.
- Christian radio reaches 93 percent of the world.
- There have been 6.5 billion viewings of the *JESUS* film.
- It is estimated that when Father Zakaria (a Christian apologist who debates Islamic clerics) is on television in the Middle East, 60 million viewers watch.
- In Iran, 7 to 9 million Persians watch satellite broadcasts of Hormoz Shariat, the "Billy Graham of Iran." That constitutes over 10 percent of the potential viewership in Iran.

So Where Is Everyone Going?

- The Great Umayyad Mosque in Damascus isn't attracting hordes of young people, and the Islamists who are trying to take Syria over are the reason. Jihad and the slaughter of innocent people is twisted and revolting to young Muslims. They can't get away from it fast enough.

- The tight borders around Islamic nations can be easily passed through via the Internet. With Facebook and Twitter, young Muslims have now connected to the world, and they are having their say. The Syrian and Egyptian protests are movements that went viral.

So what does this all mean? It means the world of Islam has an active fault line right through the middle of it. It's ready to cave in.

The world population is now 7 billion, and Islam accounts for about 20 percent of the total. Some researchers say that the high Islamic birthrate will push the Muslim portion to 25 percent within 10 years.

"But," you might say, "I thought you said Islam was imploding."

I believe it is. Just because someone is born in a Muslim family does not mean he or she will practice Islam for the rest of his or her life. The theory "once a Muslim always a Muslim" is being shot to smithereens. Islam is not winning young people through a convincing ideology. They may be threatened into staying Muslim, but many wonder, *Is there anything else? Can I truly know God personally?*

We must not ignore Muslims who are more open to the gospel now than ever before in their fourteen-century history. My wife JoAnn admits that she used to be intimidated by observant Muslim women in their garb: "Sadly, I used to look away from them as if they were invisible. I wasn't sure what to focus on even if I had wanted to talk with them. But God began to break my heart for these misunderstood women. They are marginalized and rejected by so many in America. It's probably because deep inside we wonder if they are really hiding something. *Are they terrorists? Are they wired with explosives?* How's that for believers living under a spirit of fear?

"But I know God has not called us to that kind of thinking. God had to break me of these thoughts. He eventually gave me His heart for the women of Islam. I see them through His eyes, and I am drawn to them. So now when I see Muslim women I address them and try to start a conversation. I want them to know that I see *you*, not just your burka."

Fourteen Centuries of Outreach to Muslims

Muslims have a fourteen-hundred-year history of reading the Qur'an and following the Five Pillars of Islam. So how do you convince people who wholeheartedly follow Muhammad that they've taken a wrong turn and their souls can only be saved through Jesus, not their beloved prophet? They're not likely to chuck it all just because a Christian shares the Four Spiritual Laws or some other standard evangelical presentation. Western believers often think that if Muslims can simply get the right information, they'll give up Islam and follow Jesus in a heartbeat. Not so.

There are ways, though. Over the centuries, God has raised up faith heroes who ministered to the Islamic world. In the early 1800s, Henry Martin traveled to Persia as a missionary and translated the New Testament into Farsi. A copy of his translation made it to the shah, who read it from Matthew to Revelation. Out of his experience, Martin developed seven principles for sharing Christ with Muslims, and his methods still guide missionaries today. In keeping with his motto for life, "Let me burn out for God," Martin died at the age of forty-two.

Samuel Zwemer became known as "The Apostle to Islam," and from 1890 till 1940, he ministered in the Islamic world from Bahrain to Egypt. But Zwemer found that reaching Muslims for Christ was perhaps harder than reaching any other people group. His lifelong assistant, Ruth Tucker, remarked just before Zwemer's death that for all his efforts, he probably saw fewer than a dozen conversions. Yet Zwemer believed he had fulfilled his calling and set the correct benchmark for any missions effort. The goal is not the salvation of souls but rather to bring glory to God.

I believe the combined missionary efforts since the days of Muhammad himself have been used by God to prepare a foundation for outreach today. Like prophets in the Old Testament, these saints of God did not see the fulfillment of their vision to reach throngs of Muslims for Christ. That dream would be fulfilled at a later time. And that time, I believe, is now.

Notes

Preface: Jesus and Muslims

1. See the parable of the wheat and the tares in Matthew 13. (The world *tares* comes from the King James Version.) In this parable, the wheat represents true believers. The tares represent unbelievers.

Chapter 3: Infidel Gathering

1. For more about Voice of the Martyrs, see www.persecution.com.
2. Tom White, *The Voice of the Martyrs Newsletter* (July 2011):1.

Chapter 8: Nukes, Imams, and the Underground Sheikh

1. According to a DEBKA file report (June 8, 2011), "Fordo is a well-guarded underground facility situated near the military installations surrounding the holy city of Qom and is protected by air defense missile batteries. It was burrowed deep into the side of a mountain" (www.debka.com).

Chapter 9: Clinically Impressed

1. "Dreaming of a Caliphate," *The Economist*, April 6, 2011.
2. For more information about e3, see http://www.e3partners.org/.

Intermission: The Great Awakening for Muslims

1. George Martin, "The God Who Reveals Mysteries: Dreams and World Evangelization," *Southern Baptist Journal of Theology* (Louisville, KY: Southern Baptist Theological Seminary, 2004), 8:9.

Chapter 16: Will the Real Jesus Please Stand Up?

1. http://en.wikipedia.org/wiki/List_of_Jewish_Nobel_laureates.
2. In the Qur'an, Jesus is called Isa, but for simplicity of discussion, we will call him Jesus throughout this chapter.
3. Jeff Morton, *The Two Messiahs* (Colorado Springs: Biblica, 2011), 141.
4. Rollo May in Neil T. Anderson, *Restored: Experience Life with Jesus* (Franklin, TN: e3 Resources, 2007), 11.

Chapter 20: The Man of Peace in "Boom!" Town

1. Joel C. Rosenberg, *Inside the Revolution: How the Followers of Jihad, Jefferson, and Jesus Are Battling to Dominate the Middle East and Transform the World* (Wheaton, IL: Tyndale, 2009).
2. Tom Doyle, *Breakthrough: The Return of Hope to the Middle East* (Downers Grove, IL: InterVarsity, 2009).
3. Jason Mandryk, *Operation World*, 7th ed. (Biblica Publishing, 2010), 916.
4. Heather Mercer and Dayna Curry, *Prisoners of Hope: The Story of Our Captivity and Freedom in Afghanistan* (Colorado Springs: WaterBrook, 2003).
5. "World Watch List Countries," accessed May 21, 2012, http://www.worldwatchlist.us/world-watch-list-countries.

Appendix 3: The Global Shift—Christianity Soars Ahead of Islam

1. David Garrison, *Church Planting Movements* (Peabody, BA: Wigtake Resources, 2003).

Acknowledgments

To JoAnn: What a joy it is to be married to you! I love you today more than ever. Thank you for sharing over 30 wonderful, fun-filled, exciting, unpredictable years with me. You hear God's voice and follow Him whole-heartedly. What an example you are to me, our children, and others around the world. To our Children: Shanna, Tommy, John-Mark, Lindsay, Joshua, and Sarah—What a privilege it is to be your dad. It is a very high honor. It is also a real blast! Thank you for your heart for the people of the Middle East. To the spouses—Jay, Matthew, Eleonora: We are so blessed that you have joined our family and look forward to the three yet to come! To the Grands—Emma, Ethan, and Emmet, and to the ones not yet born: May you love Jesus with all your heart, soul, and strength just like the amazing believers of *Dreams and Visions*. We thank God that He gave us the privilege seeing you grow up and grow strong in Him. I love you. Grandpa is done with the book. You want to go to Disney World?

To Dad and Mom Doyle and Mom Renda: Thank you for giving me unconditional love. Your wisdom has given our family a clear path to travel life on. "The best parents" is an understatement. You are each a gift from God! Mom, thank you for teaching me to sing songs about Jesus. He really does have the whole world in

His hand. Dad, thank you for teaching me about character and leadership, and how to hit a golf ball. Ann, thank you for loving me as your son. You have a missionary heart. To Terry and Mary Beth: You are the best sisters! Your encouragement is always perfectly timed. Thank you for cheering me on, whether it was in sports, ministry, or writing. Ed and Matthew: Since I lost my brother Mark, thank you for being one to me. To Marky: I wish I could have spent more time with you. But God wanted you in heaven with Him. How fun our brother time is going to be in the presence of Jesus! To Kathy and Larry: Thank you for loving me and welcoming me into the Renda family. You are a great blessing. To quote your mom, "I wish we all lived closer." Clark and Jane: Come visit us!

To Curtis Hail and the e3 Partners/ I Am Second Team both here and on the frontlines around the world: God's hand is on you. We live in the days of the great harvest. Jesus' message of grace and forgiveness can reach the world in our lifetime. Full speed ahead! To the MECA Team: Thank you for your love for the nations and your over-the-top efforts. Jesus brought us together to serve Him in this strategic region. I am so grateful for each of you! What an inspiration you are to me and to so many. To David Shepherd: Thank you for being a great friend! You are an awesome writing coach and advisor. Your guidance made the difference. To Greg Webster: Thank you for helping shape these real-life stories! You are an artist with words. What a pleasure to work with you. To the Thomas Nelson Team: Matt Baugher, Adria Haley, Stephanie Newton, Kristi Smith, and so many others. What a team of servants you are! It is a great blessing to write with all of you. Thank you for believing in the need to tell these "Jesus stories."